SOUL FEAST

NEIL ASTLEY is editor of Bloodaxe Books, which he founded in 1978. His books include novels, poetry collections and anthologies, most notably the Bloodaxe *Staying Alive* series: *Staying Alive* (2002), *Being Alive* (2004), *Being Human* (2011) and *Staying Human* (2011); and four collaborations with Pamela Robertson-Pearce, the DVD-anthologies *In Person: 30 Poets* (2008) and *In Person: World Poets* (2017), and the anthologies *Soul Food* (2007) and *Soul Feast* (2024). He has published two novels, *The End of My Tether* (2002/2003), which was shortlisted for the Whitbread First Novel Award, and *The Sheep Who Changed the World* (2005). He received an Eric Gregory Award for his poetry, was given a D.Litt by Newcastle University for his work with Bloodaxe Books, and in 2018 was made an Honorary Fellow of the Royal Society of Literature. He lives in Northumberland.

PAMELA ROBERTSON-PEARCE is an artist, filmmaker and translator. Her films include *IMAGO: Meret Oppenheim* (1988/1996), on the artist who made the fur-lined teacup, and *Gifted Beauty* (2000), about Surrealist women artists including Leonora Carrington and Remedios Varo. *IMAGO: Meret Oppenheim* won several awards, including the Swiss Film Board's Prize for Outstanding Quality and the Gold Apple Award at the National Educational Film and Video Festival in America. She has shown her work in solo exhibitions in New York and Provincetown (Cape Cod), and in various group shows in the US and Europe. Born in Stockholm, she grew up in Sweden, Spain and England, and then for over 20 years lived mostly in America – also working in Switzerland, Norway and Albania – before moving to Northumberland.

SOUL FEAST

NOURISHING POEMS
OF HOPE AND LIGHT

EDITED BY NEIL ASTLEY
& PAMELA ROBERTSON-PEARCE

BLOODAXE BOOKS

ISBN: 978 1 78037 706 3

First published 2024 by
Bloodaxe Books Ltd,
Eastburn,
South Park,
Hexham,
Northumberland NE46 1BS.

For Noah, always

www.bloodaxebooks.com
For further information about Bloodaxe titles
please visit our website and join our mailing list
or write to the above address for a catalogue

Supported by
**ARTS COUNCIL
ENGLAND**

Printed in Great Britain by Bell & Bain Limited, Glasgow, Scotland, on
acid-free paper sourced from mills with FSC chain of custody certification.

Contents

1. JOURNEYS

2. SOUL SEARCH

3. LIFE ON EARTH

4. ALL TOGETHER NOW

5. HOPE AND LIGHT

Packing for the Future: Instructions

LORNA CROZIER

Take the thickest socks.
Wherever you're going
you'll have to walk.

There may be water.
There may be stones.
There may be high places
you cannot go without
the hope socks bring you,
the way they hold you
to the earth.

At least one pair must be new,
must be blue as a wish
hand-knit by your mother
in her sleep.

*

Take a leather satchel,
a velvet bag and an old tin box –
a salamander painted on the lid.

This is to carry that small thing
you cannot leave. Perhaps the key

you've kept though it doesn't fit
any lock you know,
the photograph that keeps you sane,
a ball of string to lead you out
though you can't walk back
into that light.

In your bag leave room for sadness,
leave room for another language.

There may be doors nailed shut.
There may be painted windows.
There may be signs that warn you
to be gone. Take the dream
you've been having since
you were a child, the one
with open fields and the wind
sounding.

*

Mistrust no one who offers you
water from a well, a songbird's feather,
something that's been mended twice.
Always travel lighter
than the heart.

The Intimate Future

MARY O'DONNELL

The first day will startle in a paradise
of spectacle and movement. In this release
from the wintry cocoon, the long chill
over, we will forget our solitude.
Like nectar-starved butterflies, we'll cluster
together in displays of brightening wings,
velvety trims, our chitined scales and spots
trembling at the end of long starvation.

We'll fly close – so close – to one another
in drifts of prismatic colour, our patterns,
shapes, antennae, colliding, shifting,
crowding sociably to drink and drink:
such intimate nectars, proboscis-fed
to another's need, wings sugar-drowsy.

As I Go

JULIUS CHINGONO

My pot is an old paint container
I do not know
who bought it
I do not know
whose house it decorated
I picked up the empty tin
in Cemetery Lane.
My lamp, a paraffin lamp
is an empty 280ml bottle
labelled 40 per cent alcohol
I picked up the bottle in a trash bin.
My cup
is an old jam tin
I do not know who enjoyed the sweetness
I found the tin
in a storm-water drain.
My plate is a motor car hub-cap cover
I do not know
whose car it belonged to
I found a boy wheeling it, playing with it
My house is built
from plastic over cardboard
I found the plastic being blown by the wind
It's simple
I pick up my life
as I go.

Crossing

JERICHO BROWN

The water is one thing, and one thing for miles.
The water is one thing, making this bridge
Built over the water another. Walk it
Early, walk it back when the day goes dim, everyone
Rising just to find a way toward rest again.
We work, start on one side of the day
Like a planet's only sun, our eyes straight
Until the flame sinks. The flame sinks. Thank God
I'm different. I've figured and counted. I'm not crossing
To cross back. I'm set
On something vast. It reaches
Long as the sea. I'm more than a conqueror, bigger
Than bravery. I don't march. I'm the one who leaps.

If china

STANISŁAV BARAŃCAK

translated from the Polish
by MAGNUS J. KRYNSKI

If china, then only the kind
you wouldn't miss under the movers' shoes or the treads of a tank;
if a chair, then one that's not too comfortable, or
you'll regret getting up and leaving;
if clothes, then only what will fit in one suitcase;
if books, then those you know by heart;
if plans, then the ones you can give up
when it comes time for the next move,
to another street, another continent or epoch
or world:

who told you you could settle in?
who told you this or that would last forever?
didn't anyone tell you you'll never
in the world
feel at home here?

The Way It Is

WILLIAM STAFFORD

There's a thread you follow. It goes among
things that change. But it doesn't change.
People wonder about what you are pursuing.
You have to explain about the thread.
But it is hard for others to see.
While you hold it you can't get lost.
Tragedies happen; people get hurt
or die; and you suffer and get old.
Nothing you do can stop time's unfolding.
You don't ever let go of the thread.

'I drew a line...'

TOON TELLEGEN

translated from the Dutch
by JUDITH WILKINSON

I drew a line:
this far, and no further,
never will I go further than this.

When I went further,
I drew a new line,
and then another line.

The sun was shining
and everywhere I saw people,
hurried and serious,
and everyone was drawing a line,
everyone went further.

Train Ride

RUTH STONE

All things come to an end;
small calves in Arkansas,
the bend of the muddy river.
Do all things come to an end?
No, they go on forever.
They go on forever, the swamp,
the vine-choked cypress, the oaks
rattling last year's leaves,
the thump of the rails, the kite,
the still white stilted heron.
All things come to an end.
The red clay bank, the spread hawk,
the bodies riding this train,
the stalled truck, pale sunlight, the talk;
the talk goes on forever,
the wide dry field of geese,
a man stopped near his porch
to watch. Release, release;
between cold death and a fever,
send what you will, I will listen.
All things come to an end.
No, they go on forever.

Tracks

**TOMAS
TRANSTRÖMER**

*translated from the Swedish
by* ROBIN FULTON

2 A.M.: moonlight. The train has stopped
out in the middle of the plain. Far away, points of light in a town,
flickering coldly at the horizon.

As when a man has gone into a dream so deep
he'll never remember having been there
when he comes back to his room.

As when someone has gone into an illness so deep
everything his days were becomes a few flickering points, a swarm,
cold and tiny at the horizon.

The train is standing quite still.
2 A.M.: bright moonlight, few stars.

November 12

4:30 A.M.

TED KOOSER

On mornings like this, as hours before dawn
I walk the dark hall of the road
with my life creaking under my feet, I sometimes
take hold of the cold porcelain knob
of the moon, and turn it, and step into a room
warm and yellow, and take my seat
at a small wooden table with a border of painted pansies,
and wait for my mother to bring me my bowl.

We Go On

KERRY HARDIE

There's a band of black weather under the rim of the sky,
then a shimmer of light, spreading the face of the sea.

A man walks a dog and gulls drape themselves
on the unseen flow of bright air—

and it feels like everything's happened already,
and everyone's fighting to board the last plane,

though the man is still walking the dog and more gulls
settle to stud the roof of an empty shed

and maybe it's always been this way,
with all of us sure of our own redemption:

though it's dark out there, we'll still muddle through,
and it's somebody else who'll fall off the edge of the world.

Two poems

LAL DED

translated from the Kashmiri
by RANJIT HOSKOTÉ

I wore myself out, looking for myself.
No one could have worked harder to break the code.
I lost myself in myself and found a wine cellar. Nectar,
    I tell you.
There were jars and jars of the good stuff, and no one to
    drink it.

*

You won't find the Truth
by crossing your legs and holding your breath.
Daydreams won't take you through the gateway of release.
You can stir as much salt as you like in water,
it won't become the sea.

Counting, New Year's Morning, What Powers Yet Remain to Me

JANE HIRSHFIELD

The world asks, as it asks daily:
And what can you make, can you do, to change my deep-broken,
fractured?

I count, this first day of another year, what remains.
I have a mountain, a kitchen, two hands.

Can admire with two eyes the mountain,
actual, recalcitrant, shuffling its pebbles, sheltering foxes and
beetles.

Can make black-eyed peas and collards.
Can make, from last year's late-ripening persimmons, a pudding.
Can climb a stepladder, change the bulb in a track light.

For years, I woke each day first to the mountain,
then to the question.

The feet of the new sufferings followed the feet of the old,
and still they surprised.

I brought salt, brought oil, to the question. Brought sweet tea,
brought postcards and stamps. For years, each day, something.

Stone did not become apple. War did not become peace.
Yet joy still stays joy. Sequins stay sequins. Words still bespangle, bewilder.

Today, I woke without answer.

The day answers, unpockets a thought as though from a friend—

don't despair of this falling world, not yet   didn't it give you the asking

The Gift

KONA MACPHEE

Sometimes the recompense arrives
so far ahead of what you'll give
that you will fail to recognise
the reciprocity, the love

that circles in the universe:
this life a grace advanced, its knack
to meet requital with its cause –
the offering up, the giving back.

The Gift

DENISE LEVERTOV

Just when you seem to yourself
nothing but a flimsy web
of questions, you are given
the questions of others to hold
in the emptiness of your hands,
songbird eggs that can still hatch
if you keep them warm,
butterflies opening and closing themselves
in your cupped palms, trusting you not to injure
their scintillant fur, their dust.
You are given the questions of others
as if they were answers
to all you ask. Yes, perhaps
this gift is your answer.

Yeshwant Rao

ARUN KOLATKAR

Are you looking for a god?
I know a good one.
His name is Yeshwant Rao
and he's one of the best.
Look him up
when you are in Jejuri next.

Of course he's only a second class god
and his place is just outside the main temple.
Outside even of the outer wall.
As if he belonged
among the tradesmen and the lepers.

I've known gods
prettier faced
or straighter laced.
Gods who soak you for your gold.
Gods who soak you for your soul.
Gods who make you walk
on a bed of burning coal.
Gods who put a child inside your wife.
Or a knife inside your enemy.
Gods who tell you how to live your life,
double your money
or triple your land holdings.
Gods who can barely suppress a smile
as you crawl a mile for them.

Gods who will see you drown
if you won't buy them a new crown.
And although I'm sure they're all to be praised,
they're either too symmetrical
or too theatrical for my taste.

Yeshwant Rao,
mass of basalt,
bright as any post box,
the shape of protoplasm
or a king size lava pie
thrown against the wall,
without an arm, a leg
or even a single head.

Yeshwant Rao.
He's the god you've got to meet.
If you're short of a limb,
Yeshwant Rao will lend you a hand
and get you back on your feet.

Yeshwant Rao
does nothing spectacular.
He doesn't promise you the earth
or book your seat on the next rocket to heaven.
But if any bones are broken,
you know he'll mend them.

He'll make you whole in your body
and hope your spirit will look after itself.
He is merely a kind of a bone setter.
The only thing is,
as he himself has no heads, hands and feet,
he happens to understand you a little better.

'When he comes...'

TUKARAM

translated from the Marathi
by DILIP CHITRE

When He comes
Out of the blue
A meteorite
Shattering your home
Be sure
God is visiting you

When a catastrophe
Wipes you out
And nothing remains
But God and you
God is visiting you

When your language
Is stripped naked
Never to be clothed
In falsehood again
Be sure

God is visiting you

When your humanness
Is rent and riven
Never to be pieced
Together again
Be sure
God is visiting you

When you are
Beyond all hope
When you call
Nothing your own
Be sure
God is visiting you

When you are robbed
Of the whole world
And your voice
Becomes eloquent
Be sure
God is visiting you.

See how God has
Grabbed the whole of him!
Tuka is raging
Like God Himself!

The Believer

KATHLEEN OSSIP

I made a God. I called her Grace.
I said my prayers. I called them pleasure.
Pleasure her way to teach me pleasure.
Pleasure a stream and I a fish.

I made a God. I called her Grace.
I used no clay, no bronze, no iron.
I used my parts to make her whole.
And then I was part of the whole.

I found the others. I call them brave.
We laugh in the stream. We roll in the snow.
Our anger grows lilacs, our patience makes teeth.
The universe glows with oxytocin.

The Milky Way is part of the whole,
and we are part of the Milky Way.
The light makes a stream. The two streams flow.
The streams come together and we give birth.

We bathe our babies in the stream.
Babies we made and now they smile
at the God I made who I called Grace.
We say the prayers that are our pleasure.

Fabrications

DENNIS O'DRISCOLL

God is dead to the world.

But he still keeps up
           appearances. Day after
day he sets out his stall.
           Today, his special is

a sun-melt served on
           a fragrant bed of
moist cut-grass; yesterday,
           a misty-eyed moon,

a blister pack of stars.
           Lakes and mountains
are standard stock;
           flowers and birds

in season. The avocado,
           shining knight, and the
tightly-swathed cabbage
           remain evergreens.

Odd years, for novelty,
           he tweaks the weather
patterns, brings forward
           spring by weeks, lets

the crocus's petal-
        pronged attack on
frozen ground begin
        ahead of schedule:

softening air's frosty
        disposition; making good
the winter's blemishes.
        Special effects – flash floods,

meteor showers clashing
        overhead, the cradle cap
of a lunar eclipse – are reserved
        for visionary interludes.

Not that it matters;
        nothing is sacred any more;
no one much takes him
        at his word, buys his

version of the story, seeks
        corroboration of his
claims; the steeple's beak
        no longer nourishes its flock.

People idly browse his wares,
             knock back samples
of coconut milk, add Gruyère
             to a quiche, test the texture

of the beach sand with bare feet,
             before resorting to the soft
option of a recliner: a pew from
             which to worship the sun's heat.

Blowing hot or cold
             as mood or precedent
dictates, he offers further
             cryptic clues – a flatfish

sporting two left eyes,
             a tree that moults fur catkins,
an orchid mimicking a fly,
             a blackbird whose bill

is toucan orange, a baby battling
             with acute leukaemia,
a cow resting among buttercups
             like a whale awash in plankton.

But few make the link,
 speculate enough
to track these fabrications
 back to source.

He starts from scratch each day
 with new creations: drafting
a summer dawn, he permits
 the sun – only minimally

resisted by the mist, a token
 skirmish – to assume control,
making for profligate horizons,
 lofty skies, beyond which

other universes stack up,
 dangled in suspense,
the way a mountain lake
 is cupped in sandstone hands.

And every pulsing star will live
 according to his lights,
individually illumined,
 nimbus visible to the eye.

I Was Never Able to Pray

EDWARD HIRSCH

Wheel me down to the shore
where the lighthouse was abandoned
and the moon tolls in the rafters.

Let me hear the wind paging through the trees
and see the stars flaring out, one by one,
like the forgotten faces of the dead.

I was never able to pray,
but let me inscribe my name
in the book of waves

and then stare into the dome
of a sky that never ends
and see my voice sail into the night.

Prayer

*(to my mother,
Anna Picchi)*

GIORGIO CAPRONI

*translated from the Italian
by* PETER SIRR

Go lightly, soul, go
to Livorno
with flickering
candle, at night time
and look around
and if you have time
search high and low,
let me know
if by any chance
Anna Picchi
is among the living still.

Only today,
disappointed
I returned from Livorno
but you, so
much sharper than me,
you'll remember
the blouse she'd wear
with the ruby set
in the little gold snake
and how it seemed to blur
as you looked at it.

Be clever, my soul,
and go
in search of her.
You know what I'd give
to meet her on the street.

Prayer

**ARUNDHATHI
SUBRAMANIAM**

May things stay the way they are
in the simplest place you know.

May the shuttered windows
keep the air as cool as bottled jasmine.
May you never forget to listen
to the crumpled whisper of sheets
that mould themselves to your sleeping form.
May the pillows always be silvered
with cat-down and the muted percussion
of a lover's breath.
May the murmur of the wall clock
continue to decree that your providence
run ten minutes slow.

May nothing be disturbed
in the simplest place you know
for it is here in the foetal hush
that blueprints dissolve
and poems begin,
and faith spreads like the hum of crickets,
faith in a time
when maps shall fade,
nostalgia cease
and the vigil end.

Poem Written in a Copy of 'Beowulf'

JORGE LUIS BORGES

translated from the Spanish
by ALASTAIR REID

At various times I have asked myself what reasons
moved me to study while my night came down,
without particular hope of satisfaction,
the language of the blunt-tongued Anglo-Saxons.
Used up by the years my memory
loses its grip on words that I have vainly
repeated and repeated. My life in the same way
weaves and unweaves its weary history.
Then I tell myself: it must be that the soul
has some secret sufficient way of knowing
that it is immortal, that its vast encompassing
circle can take in all, accomplish all.
Beyond my anxiety and beyond this writing
the universe waits, inexhaustible, inviting.

A Saxon Primer

Más allá de este afán y de este verso
me aguarda inagotable el universo.
— BORGES

PETER SIRR

Then I think of Borges going blind,
of what he said about the soul.
He was trying to understand
why a man who was losing the world
would seek out swords and monsters,
blunt-voiced Saxons in the mead hall.

It's that the soul must know it's immortal,
he said, and its hungry turning circle
takes everything in, achieves all that's possible.
There's a kind of secret knowledge
enfolds us, reaches everything we do
or else all we do is the knowledge and the soul.

Beyond all this, the sweated grammar,
the effort to know one thing after another,
on the other side of the poem the universe is waiting,
patient and inexhaustible. Time and again
the light keeps fading from what we love
though we turn and turn to it, singing

to blunt the darkness, to fold the light back in.

Soul Keeping Company

LUCIE BROCK-BOIDO

I sat with her in keeping company
All through the affliction of the night, keeping

Soul constant, a second self. Earth is heavy
And I made no wish, save being

Merely magical. I am magical
No more. This, I well remember well.

In the sweet thereafter the impress
Of the senses will be tattooed to

The whole world ravelling in the clemency
Of an autumn of Octobers, all that bounty

Bountiful and the oaks specifically
Afire as everything dies off, inclining

To the merciful. I would have made of my body
A body to protect her, anything to keep

Her well & here – in the soul's suite
Before five tons of earth will bear

On her, stay here
Soul, in the good night of my company.

The hours between washing and the well
Of burial are the soul's most troubled time.

Soul Washing

ADRIANA LISBOA

*(for my brother
and my sister)*

*translated from the Portuguese
by* ALISON ENTREKEN

The soul must be washed by hand.
Not that its fabric is delicate,
or that its colours run. On the contrary,
the soul is coarse and the only way to get it clean
is to wash it by hand. Take
a bar of laundry soap – the cheapest will do.
Forget bleach, fabric softener,
no soul needs that.
Let it soak for a while
to remove stubborn dirt, grease,
mud, tomato sauce stains.
Then rub it in the sink,
wring it out and hang it in the sun. No
ironing is required. Washed like this,
the soul can be worn
for many years to come,
the ideal uniform for this school
of obstinacy that is the body,
that is the world.

Question

MAY SWENSON

Body my house
my horse my hound
what will I do
when you are fallen

Where will I sleep
How will I ride
What will I hunt

Where can I go
without my mount
all eager and quick
How will I know
in thicket ahead
is danger or treasure
when Body my good
bright dog is dead

How will it be
to lie in the sky
without roof or door
and wind for an eye

With cloud for shift
how will I hide?

O Taste and See

DENISE LEVERTOV

The world is
not with us enough.
O taste and see

the subway Bible poster said,
meaning **The Lord**, meaning
if anything all that lives
to the imagination's tongue,

grief, mercy, language.
tangerine, weather, to
breathe them, bite,
savor, chew, swallow, transform

into our flesh our
deaths, crossing the street, plum, quince,
living in the orchard and being

hungry, and plucking
the fruit.

Imaginary Conversation

LINDA PASTAN

You tell me to live each day
as if it were my last. This is in the kitchen
where before coffee I complain
of the day ahead – that obstacle race
of minutes and hours,
grocery stores and doctors.

But why the last? I ask. Why not
live each day as if it were the first –
all raw astonishment, Eve rubbing
her eyes awake that first morning,
the sun coming up
like an ingénue in the east?

You grind the coffee
with the small roar of a mind
trying to clear itself. I set
the table, glance out the window
where dew has baptised every
living surface.

Yes

MURIEL RUKEYSER

It's like a tap-dance
Or a new pink dress,
A shit-naive feeling
Saying Yes.

Some say Good morning
Some say God bless –
Some say Possibly
Some say Yes.

Some say Never
Some say Unless
It's stupid and lovely
To rush into Yes.

What can it mean?
It's just like life,
One thing to you
One to your wife.

Some go local
Some go express
Some can't wait
To answer Yes.

Some complain
Of strain and stress
The answer may be
No for Yes.

Some like failure
Some like success
Some like Yes Yes
Yes Yes Yes.

Open your eyes,
Dream but don't guess.
Your biggest surprise
Comes after Yes.

To Be Alive

GREGORY ORR

To be alive: not just the carcass
But the spark.
That's crudely put, but...

If we're not supposed to dance,
Why all this music?

Addiction to an Old Mattress

ROSEMARY TONKS

No, this is not my life, thank God…
…worn out like this, and crippled by brain-fag;
Obsessed first by one person, and then
(Almost at once) most horribly besotted by another;
These Februaries, full of draughts and cracks,
They belong to the people in the streets, the others
Out there – haberdashers, writers of menus.

Salt breezes! Bolsters from Istanbul!
Barometers, full of contempt, controlling moody isobars.
Sumptuous tittle-tattle from a summer crowd
That's fed on lemonades and matinées. And seas
That float themselves about from place to place, and then
Spend *hours* – just moving some clear sleets across glass stones.
Yalta: deck-chairs in Asia's gold cake; thrones.

Meanwhile… I live on… powerful, disobedient,
Inside their draughty haberdasher's climate,
With these people…who are going to obsess me,
Potatoes, dentists, people I hardly know, it's unforgivable
For this is not my life
But theirs, that I am living.
And I wolf, bolt, gulp it down, day after day.

Dear Life

MAYA C. POPA

I can't undo all I have done to myself,
what I have let an appetite for love do to me.

I have wanted all the world, its beauties
and its injuries; some days,
I think that is punishment enough.

Often, I received more than I'd asked,

which is how this works – you fish in open water
ready to be wounded on what you reel in.

Throwing it back was a nightmare.
Throwing it back and seeing my own face

as it disappeared into the dark water.

Catching my tongue suddenly on metal,
spitting the hook into my open palm.

Dear life: I feel that hook today most keenly.

Would you loosen the line – you'll listen

if I ask you,

if you are the sort of life I think you are.

With Only One Life

MARIN SORESCU

translated from the Romanian
by IOANA RUSSELL-GEBBETT
with D.J. ENRIGHT

Hold with both hands
The tray of every day
And pass in turn
Along this counter.

There is enough sun
For everybody.
There is enough sky,
And there is moon enough.

The earth gives off the smell
Of luck, of happiness, of glory,
Which tickles your nostrils
Temptingly.

So don't be miserly,
Live after your own heart.
The prices are derisory.

For instance, with only one life
You can acquire
The most beautiful woman,
Plus a biscuit.

Watermelon Man

JOHN McCULLOGH

Excuse me while I walk into the nearest wall.
Don't worry but I'll probably fall off the pier.
I need crash mats around me always,

                              flung about as I am
by statements, ditties, smells.
                              My head is a meteorite
falling horizontally, my legs a tall calamity
on the loose,

            chaotic as escaped giraffes.

I stumble into a market stall and demolish
its parsnip museum, create an everywhere of celery.
Tramping beside a row of houses that are different shades,
each bar of colour slams forward and dizzies me
so for a second I see nothing else.

                        Lilac! Magenta! Blue!
It's like being attacked by my first xylophone.
A musical disaster, but rather fun.

                        Yes, keep doing it, world.
Rearrange me. Keep tripping me up as I try for normal,
attempt to lug this heart unwieldy as a watermelon,
dropped and salvaged each day, but firmly sweet.

Love Poem with Apologies for My Appearance

ADA LIMÓN

Sometimes, I think you get the worst
of me. The much-loved loose forest-green
sweatpants, the long bra-less days, hair
knotted and uncivilised, a shadowed brow
where the devilish thoughts do their hoofed
dance on the brain. I'd like to say this means
I love you, the stained white cotton T-shirt,
the tears, pistachio shells, the mess of orange
peels on my desk, but it's different than that.
I move in this house with you, the way I move
in my mind, unencumbered by beauty's cage.
I do like I do in the tall grass, more animal-me
than much else. I'm wrong, it is that I love you,
but it's more that when you say it back, lights
out, a cold wind through curtains, for maybe
the first time in my life, I believe it.

Path

JACK HIRSCHMAN

Go to your broken heart.
If you think you don't have one, get one.
To get one, be sincere.
Learn sincerity of intent by letting
life enter because you're helpless, really,
to do otherwise.
Even as you try escaping, let it take you
and tear you open
like a letter sent,
like a sentence inside
you've waited for all your life
though you've committed nothing.
Let it send you up.
Let it break you, heart.
Broken-heartedness is the beginning
of all real reception.
The ear of humility hears beyond the gates.
See the gates opening.
Feel your hands going akimbo on your hips,
your mouth opening like a womb
giving birth to your voice for the first time.
Go singing whirling into the glory
of being ecstatistically simple.
Write the poem.

A Brief for the Defense

JACK GILBERT

Sorrow everywhere. Slaughter everywhere. If babies
are not starving someplace, they are starving
somewhere else. With flies in their nostrils.
But we enjoy our lives because that's what God wants.
Otherwise the mornings before summer dawn would not
be made so fine. The Bengal tiger would not
be fashioned so miraculously well. The poor women
at the fountain are laughing together between
the suffering they have known and the awfulness
in their future, smiling and laughing while somebody
in the village is very sick. There is laughter
every day in the terrible streets of Calcutta,
and the women laugh in the cages of Bombay.
If we deny our happiness, resist our satisfaction,
we lessen the importance of their deprivation.
We must risk delight. We can do without pleasure,
but not delight. Not enjoyment. We must have
the stubbornness to accept our gladness in the ruthless
furnace of this world. To make injustice the only
measure of our attention is to praise the Devil.
If the locomotive of the Lord runs us down,
we should give thanks that the end had magnitude.
We must admit there will be music despite everything.
We stand at the prow again of a small ship
anchored late at night in the tiny port
looking over to the sleeping island: the waterfront
is three shuttered cafés and one naked light burning.

To hear the faint sound of oars in the silence as a rowboat
comes slowly out and then goes back is truly worth
all the years of sorrow that are to come.

The Thing Is

ELLEN BASS

to love life, to love it even
when you have no stomach for it
and everything you've held dear
crumbles like burnt paper in your hands,
your throat filled with the silt of it.
When grief sits with you, its tropical heat
thickening the air, heavy as water
more fit for gills than lungs;
when grief weights you down like your own flesh
only more of it, an obesity of grief,
you think, *How can a body withstand this?*
Then you hold life like a face
between your palms, a plain face,
no charming smile, no violet eyes,
and you say, yes, I will take you
I will love you, again.

Any Common Desolation

ELLEN BASS

can be enough to make you look up
at the yellowed leaves of the apple tree, the few
that survived the rains and frost, shot
with late afternoon sun. They glow a deep
orange-gold against a blue so sheer, a single bird
would rip it like silk. You may have to break
your heart, but it isn't nothing
to know even one moment alive. The sound
of an oar in an oarlock or a ruminant
animal tearing grass. The smell of grated ginger.
The ruby neon of the liquor store sign.
Warm socks. You remember your mother,
her precision a ceremony, as she gathered
the white cotton, slipped it over your toes,
drew up the heel, turned the cuff. A breath
can uncoil as you walk across your own muddy yard,
the big dipper pouring night down over you, and everything
you dread, all you can't bear, dissolves
and, like a needle slipped into your vein –
that sudden rush of the world.

Love Is a Place

JOAN MARGARIT

translated from the Catalan
by ANNA CROWE

From my seat on the train I gaze at the landscape
and suddenly, fleetingly, a vineyard goes by
which is the lightning-flash of some truth.
It would be a mistake to alight from the train
because then the vineyard would vanish.
Love is a place, and there is always something
that reveals it to me: a distant field,
a conductor's empty stand with only a rose on it,
and the musicians playing on their own.
Your room as day was breaking.
And, of course, the singing of those birds
in the cemetery, one morning in June.
Love is a place.
It endures beyond everything: from there we come.
And it's the place where life remains.

A Cedary Fragrance

JANE HIRSHFIELD

Even now,
decades after,
I wash my face with cold water –

Not for discipline,
nor memory,
nor the icy, awakening slap,

but to practise
choosing
to make the unwanted wanted.

Saint Animal

CHASE TWICHELL

Suddenly it was clear to me –
I was something I hadn't been before.
It was as if the animal part of my being

had reached some kind of maturity that gave it
authority, and had begun to use it.

I thought about death for two years.
My animal flailed and tore at its cage
till I let it go. I watched it

drift out into the easy eddies of twilight
and then veer off, not knowing me.

I'm not a bird but I'm inhabited by a spirit
that's uplifting me. It's my animal, my saint
and soldier, my flame of yearning,

come back to tell me
what it was like to be without me.

Little Prayer

MONA ARSHI

It's me
    again.
This time I'm a wren.

Last time I
    was the first
white sap.

Don't blow away
        the fruit flies
but visit my

pockets of blue-black
        pain. Little prayer
I am still here

hunkered down
        with the worm-casts
blind song

shrinking in
        my scratchy
after-feathers.

Listening

WILLIAM STAFFORD

My father could hear a little animal step,
or a moth in the dark against the screen,
and every far sound called the listening out
into places where the rest of us had never been.

More spoke to him from the soft wild night
than came to our porch for us on the wind;
we would watch him look up and his face go keen
till the walls of the world flared, widened.

My father heard so much that we still stand
inviting the quiet by turning the face,
waiting for a time when something in the night
will touch us too from that other place.

Wonder

TUVIA RUEBNER

translated from the Hebrew
by RACHEL TZVIA BACK

If after everything that has happened
you can still hear the blackbird,
the tufted lark at dawn, the bulbul and the honey-bird –
don't be surprised that happiness is watching the clouds
    being wind-carried away,
is drinking morning coffee, being able to execute all the
    body's needs
is walking along the paths without a cane
and seeing the burning colours of sunset.

A human being can bear almost everything
and no one knows when and where
happiness will overcome him.

A Spider

JEONG HO-SEUNG

translated from the Korean
by BROTHER ANTHONY OF TAIZÉ
& SUSAN HWANG

Early one morning
as I was walking up the road to Baekdam-sa Temple,
all the tears I have ever shed in life were hanging
on the spiders' webs strung from branch to branch.
One great spider,
who'd been approaching in a hurry, eager to gobble up
　　my tears,
was now, hands joined
in the morning sunlight,
silently
saying grace.

The Supple Deer

JANE HIRSHFIELD

The quiet opening
between fence strands
perhaps eighteen inches.

Antlers to hind hooves,
four feet off the ground,
the deer poured through.

No tuft of the coarse white belly hair left behind.

I don't know how a stag turns
into a stream, an arc of water.
I have never felt such accurate envy.

Not of the deer:

To be that porous, to have such largeness pass through me.

The Envoy

JANE HIRSHFIELD

One day in that room, a small rat.
Two days later, a snake.

Who, seeing me enter,
whipped the long stripe of his
body under the bed,
then curled like a docile house-pet.

I don't know how either came or left.
Later, the flashlight found nothing.

For a year I watched
as something – terror? happiness? grief? –
entered and then left my body.

Not knowing how it came in,
Not knowing how it went out.

It hung where words could not reach it.
It slept where light could not go.
Its scent was neither snake nor rat,
neither sensualist nor ascetic.

There are openings in our lives
of which we know nothing.

Through them
the belled herds travel at will,
long-legged and thirsty, covered with foreign dust.

The Substitute Sky

LYNNE WYCHERLEY

Each day we stare at screens,
a sly fluorescence, a not-quite sky
where swarms of data
aggregate and fly

while unseen cloud-and-sunlight
walks the grass, gold shoes
then grey, and beech and oak,
the green-leaved angels, pray.

Pilots of pixel storms,
what do we bring? Less talk,
less laughter, less sun on our skins;
our lives on hold, our children wired in.

Core addiction: captive eyes.
Outside the real world breathes, and dies.

Postscript

MARIE HOWE

What we did to the earth, we did to our daughters
one after the other.

What we did to the trees, we did to our elders
stacked in their wheelchairs by the lunchroom door.

What we did to our daughters, we did to our sons
calling out for their mothers.

What we did to the trees, what we did to the earth,
we did to our sons, to our daughters.

What we did to the cow, to the pig, to the lamb,
we did to the earth, butchered and milked it.

Few of us knew what the bird calls meant
or what the fires were saying.

We took of earth and took and took, and the earth
seemed not to mind

until one of our daughters shouted: *it was right
in front of you, right in front of your eyes*

and you didn't see.
The air turned red.   The ocean grew teeth.

4. ALL TOGETHER NOW

They Spoke to Me of People, and of Humanity

FERNANDO PESSOA

translated from the Portuguese by RICHARD ZENITH

They spoke to me of people, and of humanity.
But I've never seen people, or humanity.
I've seen various people, astonishingly dissimilar,
Each separated from the next by an unpeopled space.

This Beautiful Bubble

VINCENT KATZ

I love this bubble,
Everyone takes the subway, and you can look up,
And look at all the people, and each one is different,
And they *look* different, and each one has a story, and
    suddenly,
You are awake and want to know each story, only you can't,
Don't have time, they don't, don't want to maybe.

But some you do, you glean, you approximate yourself to
    something of them,
Like the beautiful, chestnut-skinned woman, who, leaning,
Listened to the announcer before getting in, and, confused,
    because the 2 was called a 5,
Asked advice, and three people responded,
Explaining in their different ways, some of them silent,
Eyes met with approval, warmth only subway-known,
Among equals, fellow travelers, denizens;

She sat and smiled, and looking at an infant,
Smiled more, her hair was a flag of self-joy too,
She was real, at ease among people.
The rule is: to speak.
Make contact, and you will find more people than you
    thought.

But back to our bubble. It is everywhere around us.
Everywhere, walking in the city, you are seeing people,
All different kinds, shapes, sizes, the best education
You can give a child is to bring them up inside this
Beautiful bubble. I complain, but I'll never leave.
I feed off the looks, the stories, the hungering here.

I'm aware, we're all aware, what goes on outside the bubble.
We're not stupid. We just thought people outside the bubble wanted
    the same thing:
To live as variously as possible.
Or, put another way: I am the least difficult of men.

All I want is boundless love.
It took us sixty years or so to understand
What the word 'boundless' meant.
And now we know.

Gate A-4

NAOMI SHIHAB NYE

Wandering around the Albuquerque Airport Terminal, after learning my flight had been detained four hours, I heard an announcement: 'If anyone in the vicinity of Gate A-4 understands any Arabic, please come to the gate immediately.' Well – one pauses these days. Gate A-4 was my own gate. I went there.

An older woman in full traditional Palestinian embroidered dress, just like my grandma wore, was crumpled to the floor, wailing loudly. 'Help,' said the Flight Agent. 'Talk to her. What is her problem? We told her the flight was going to be late and she did this.' I stooped to put my arm around the woman and spoke haltingly. *'Shu dow-a, Shu-bid-uck Habibti? Stani schway, Min fadlick, Shu-bit-se-wee?'* The minute she heard any words she knew, however poorly used, she stopped crying. She thought the flight had been cancelled entirely. She needed to be in El Paso for major medical treatment the next day. I said, 'You're fine, you'll get there, who's picking you up? Let's call him.' We called her son, I spoke with him in English, saying I would stay with his mother till we got on the plane.

She talked to him. Then we called her other sons just for fun. Then we called my dad and he and she spoke for a while in Arabic and found out of course they had ten shared friends. Then I thought just for the heck of it why not call some Palestinian poets I know and let them chat with her?

This all took up two hours. She was laughing a lot by then. Telling about her life, patting my knee, answering questions. She had pulled a sack of homemade *mamool* cookies – little powdered sugar crumbly mounds stuffed with dates and nuts – from her bag – and was offering them to all the women at the gate. To my amazement, not a single woman declined one. It was like a sacrament. The traveller from Argentina, the mom from California, the lovely woman from Laredo – we were all covered with the same powdered sugar. And smiling. There is no better cookie.

And then the airline broke out free apple juice from huge coolers and two little girls from our flight ran around serving it and they were covered with powdered sugar too. And I noticed my new best friend – by now we were holding hands – had a potted plant poking out of her bag, some medicinal thing, with green furry leaves. Such an old country travelling tradition. Always carry a plant. Always stay rooted to somewhere. And I looked around that gate of late and weary ones and thought, this is the world I want to live in. The shared world. Not a single person in that gate – once the crying of confusion stopped – seemed apprehensive about any other person. They took the cookies. I wanted to hug all those other women too. This can still happen anywhere. Not everything is lost.

How to Cut a Pomegranate

IMTIAZ DHARKER

'Never,' said my father,
'Never cut a pomegranate
through the heart. It will weep blood.
Treat it delicately, with respect.

Just slit the upper skin across four quarters.
This is a magic fruit,
so when you split it open, be prepared
for the jewels of the world to tumble out,
more precious than garnets,
more lustrous than rubies,
lit as if from inside.
Each jewel contains a living seed.
Separate one crystal.
Hold it up to catch the light.
Inside is a whole universe.
No common jewel can give you this.'

Afterwards, I tried to make necklaces
of pomegranate seeds.
The juice spurted out, bright crimson,
and stained my fingers, then my mouth.

I didn't mind. The juice tasted of gardens
I had never seen, voluptuous
with myrtle, lemon, jasmine,
and alive with parrots' wings.

The pomegranate reminded me
that somewhere I had another home.

Crab-apples

IMTIAZ DHARKER

My mother picked crab-apples
off the Glasgow apple trees
and pounded them with chillis
to change
her homesickness
into green chutney.

Lives

JOHN KOETHE

We have them, and live and think about them,
But then, what *are* they? Some seem like
Bigger deals than the rest, like those of big enchiladas
Or the CEOs of banks too big to fail, but why? Some seem
Meaningful for their commitments and accomplishments,
As no doubt they are, though most are unexceptional
And ordinary, and just fine for that. They're all equal
In value, but what that means is difficult to say:
That each one matters more than anything
To whoever's life it is, though each is barely real
To anyone else? The world exists before and after it,
Yet while it breathes it *is* the world, *its* world.
Whenever I attempt to gesture at it, all I find are words
For where I am: this room, this place I live. Stay with me
I want to say, yet it can't, not because it's unreal,
But because I am. Is what I want to say instead
That everything comes down to lives? The thought
Is true enough, but it's a way of feeling, not explaining,
Of poetry rather than a paper. They're real enough I guess,
Just 'metaphysically thin'. But each of them is everything.

After Someone's Death

**TOMAS
TRANSTRÖMER**

*translated from the Swedish
by* ROBIN FULTON

Once there was a shock
which left behind a long pale glimmering comet's tail.
It contains us. It makes TV pictures blurred.
It deposits itself as cold drops on the aerials.

You can still shuffle along on skis in the winter sun
among groves where last year's leaves still hang.
They are like pages torn from old telephone directories –
the subscribers' names are eaten up by the cold.

It is still beautiful to feel your heart throbbing.
But often the shadow feels more real than the body.
The samurai looks insignificant
beside his armour of black dragon-scales.

Maybe

TAHA MUHAMMAD ALI

translated from the Arabic
by PETER COLE, YAHJA HIJAZI
& GABRIEL LEVIN

Last night
in my dream
I saw I would die.
I saw death
eye to eye
and felt it –
was there inside it.
The truth is –
I've never known
before
that death
through most of its stages
would flow so easily:
a white, warm,
wide, and pleasant torpor,
a soothing sensation of lethargy.

Generally speaking,
there was neither
pain nor fear;
maybe
our excessive fear
of death
is rooted
in an intense
escalation of desire
for life.

Maybe.

But in my death
the one thing
I can't describe
is the sudden shiver
that comes across us
when we know for certain we're dying,
that soon our loved ones will vanish,
that we will not see them ever again,
or even be able to think of them.

'Good creatures...'

A.E. HOUSMAN

Good creatures, do you love your lives
    And have you ears for sense?
Here is a knife like other knives,
    That cost me eighteen pence.

I need but stick it in my heart
    And down will come the sky,
And earth's foundations will depart
    And all you folk will die.

Alone

TOMAS TRANSTRÖMER

translated from the Swedish
by ROBIN FULTON

I

One evening in February I came near to dying here.
The car skidded sideways on the ice, out
on the wrong side of the road. The approaching cars –
their lights – closed in.

My name, my girls, my job
broke free and were left silently behind
further and further away. I was anonymous
like a boy in a playground surrounded by enemies.

The approaching traffic had huge lights.
They shone on me while I pulled at the wheel
in a transparent terror that floated like egg white.
The seconds grew – there was space in them –
they grew as big as hospital buildings.

You could almost pause
and breathe out for a while
before being crushed.

Then something caught: a helping grain of sand
or a wonderful gust of wind. The car broke free
and scuttled smartly right over the road.
A post shot up and cracked – a sharp clang – it
flew away in the darkness.

Then – stillness. I sat back in my seat-belt
and saw someone coming through the whirling snow
to see what had become of me.

II   I have been walking for a long time
on the frozen Östergötland fields.
I have not seen a single person.

In other parts of the world
there are people who are born, live and die
in a perpetual crowd.

To be always visible – to live
in a swarm of eyes –
a special expression must develop.
Face coated with clay.

The murmuring rises and falls
while they divide up among themselves
the sky, the shadows, the sand grains.

I must be alone
ten minutes in the morning
and ten minutes in the evening.
– Without a programme.

Everyone is queuing at everyone's door.

Many.

One.

To Daffodils

JEONG HO-SEUNG

translated from the Korean
by BROTHER ANTHONY
OF TAIZÉ
& SUSAN HWANG

Don't cry.
To be lonely is to be human.
To go on living is to endure loneliness.
Do not wait in vain for the phone call that never comes.
When snow falls, walk on snowy paths,
when rain falls, walk on rainy paths.
A black-breasted longbill is watching you from the bed of reeds.
Sometimes even God is so lonely he weeps.
Birds perch on branches because they are lonely
and you are sitting beside the stream because you are lonely.
The hill's shadow comes down to the village once a day
            because it, too, is lonely.
And a bell's chime resounds because it, too, is lonely.

Some Meanings of Silence

SANDRA McPHERSON

It has the last word so many times.
One takes his journey or performs his experiment
then arrives at silence,
apparently
a happy ending.
Silence at its most literal I experienced once
in a northern forest.
I marvelled at it and felt misanthropic.
When bark fell or some buzzy flyer aimed by,
how exact.
Other silences just clutter the picture.
They mean 'empty' not 'clear'.
They imply 'flat' not 'tranquil'.
They say, 'Step easily out this door, I'll carry on.'
In the silence I know, I hear
how noisy my head is
and I shift toward conduct most efficient
at the still centres.
Snow knows this,
moulds and mosses and mushrooms work this way.

Silence shapes out from inside,
it is not a way out,
not for the fatigued.
Peace may be the world widest awake, creation to be awake in.
The automobiles never cease on the highway below me.

FROM

For the Break-up of a Relationship

JOHN O'DONOHUE

This is the time to be slow,
Lie low to the wall
Until the bitter weather passes.

Try, as best you can, not to let
The wire brush of doubt
Scrape from your heart
All sense of yourself
And your hesitant light.

If you remain generous,
Time will come good;
And you will find your feet
Again on fresh pastures of promise,
Where the air will be kind
And blushed with beginning.

The Art of Disappearing

NAOMI SHIHAB NYE

When they say Don't I know you?
say no.

When they invite you to the party
remember what parties are like
before answering.

Someone telling you in a loud voice
they once wrote a poem.
Greasy sausage balls on a paper plate.
Then reply.

If they say We should get together
say why?

It's not that you don't love them any more.
You're trying to remember something
too important to forget.
Trees. The monastery bell at twilight.
Tell them you have a new project.
It will never be finished.

When someone recognises you in a grocery store
nod briefly and become a cabbage.
When someone you haven't seen in ten years
appears at the door,
don't start singing him all your new songs.
You will never catch up.

Walk around feeling like a leaf.
Know you could tumble any second.
Then decide what to do with your time.

Lumberjack Diary

LEE YOUNG-JU

translated from the Korean
by JAE KIM

I didn't know how to draw this myth whose beginning is filled with darkness, so I drew a house on a blank page. The universe doesn't have any use for doors of course. We wanted to build a house because everything was open. Since we're fragile, we can't make sense of a place where backward is forward and up and down mean little. To be natural means to be able to show ourselves, of our own accord. As nothing but shadows moulded out of light and darkness, we can neither touch sorrows nor embrace joys. As we are, we can't do anything. After sending you the Bible verse that says everything turns upside down in the moments before the world ends, I erased the confessions I'd written all over my desk. In this vastness, I doubt any signal could reach you. They say a disaster is a star being destroyed. Stardust will fall and show itself on its own. The old ones, who could touch and feel shapeless things, grieved when they saw the stardust. We put up a roof and pray that the souls of those who disappeared visit us. We pray they rest their shining bodies on the roof and prepare a large pot of porridge for us. Is the tragedy impossible to explain because this is how it manifests itself? Using a long saw, we cut down a tree. Let's make a frame. We're shadows slipping in through the window. We let the hot red bean porridge drip to the ground.

Shoulders

NAOMI SHIHAB NYE

A man crosses the street in rain,
stepping gently, looking two times north and south:
because his son is asleep on his shoulder.

No car must splash him.
No car drive too near to his shadow.

This man carries the world's most sensitive cargo
but he's not marked.
Nowhere does his jacket say FRAGILE,
HANDLE WITH CARE.

His ear fills up with breathing.
He hears the hum of a boy's dream
deep inside him.

We're not going to be able
to live in this world
if we're not willing to do what he's doing
with one another.

The road will only be wide.
The rain will never stop falling.

Instead of Dying

LAUREN HALDEMAN

Instead of dying, you move in with us. We fix the basement up with a shower & a small area for your bed & you come to live. I help you carry boxes down the stairs. We set up your record player. We hang up your old poster from 5th grade that says 'Save the Wolves'. Once a week, you make grilled cheese for us in the upstairs kitchen. Instead of dying, instead of being stabbed on the street in Denver, instead of bleeding to death surrounded by strangers neither you nor I will ever meet, instead of all that, you get a job at the local grocery store, stocking the shelves, watering the produce: collards, endive, grapefruit. Your face stays your face & your pain gets better & you swim at the Rec Centre in the early light of spring & you are so not not not dead.

Instead of dying, they inject you with sunlight & you live. It is a highly experimental process developed in the deep caverns of Luray, where a fluid from the crevices of the previous earth is found to contain a slow conglomerate of sunlight. Scientists discover they can separate the plasma into a medicinal dose, a shot of which can bring a boy back from death after being stabbed three times in the chest. *The Belt of Orion*, they call it. And it works. The moment the needle goes into your arm, you open your eyes. The bright light enters your bloodstream. And we thank the doctors and the ambulance drivers and even the man who did this to you, since he provided us with the opportunity to infuse you with infinite illumination.

a small book of questions: chapter VII

CHEN CHEN

What would you say if you could?

She asks about the dog before she asks about the boyfriend.

She doesn't ask about him. She does this for a year.

Will do this for years. Even after the boyfriend & I move back to the Northeast. Even when we're living ten minutes away & she comes to our apartment with an ugly vase I suspect she is regifting. I accept it because she has also brought a large container full of green beans fried with garlic. She looks at the dog, seems to have an easier time looking at the dog, than looking at the boyfriend, the boyfriends, us. I want to say, Mom, look. *Ask*

about us. She asks about the dog.

(How's his hair? Everywhere?)

Then I remember—about a year before we're ten minutes away, we come over from Rochester. We join my brother's college graduation lunch at Mu Lan in Waltham. & we're part of a party of six, eating as a party of twelve. The boyfriend goes to the bathroom. She goes back to the dishes, which are somehow not finished, yet. She's not. She's picking up two magnificently crispy scallion pancakes—their full magnificence held between her chopsticks, her skilfully nonchalant grip—& then she's placing them on the boyfriend's plate. She looks at me. Says, *For him.*

Maybe she is asking about us by asking about the dog.

> (Or she asks about the dog because he is cuter than
> the boyfriend, cuter than the son, we might as well
> all be regifted vases compared to the dog.)

She says, *He likes the pancakes, he should have more.*

& what would she say if she could

say, be more? & what am I looking for, exactly? Do I look at
her, the way she would like? Have I said *I love you* recently—
the exact words, yes, but what about the exact foods? Couldn't
we ask each other for more?

At the least, I want to remember better. Earlier this summer,
she asks if he's coming over with me, for the 4th. She's making
hotdogs & hamburgers, wants to know if she needs to make
veggie burgers. For the boyfriend. *For him.* For some reason I
think dinner, not lunch, so say, *Sure, we'll both come once he
finishes with work.*

She's disappointed when he can't come. She doesn't say dis-
appointed. Says, *Take*

*the veggie one*s, & puts them in a large container, & that into a very large bag. Always these containers & bags, large & small & larger. She probably has something large enough, vast enough to carry all the hair the dog sheds, will ever shed.

> (I want to remember better.
> But I want more, more of the
> better to remember.)

She sighs in the midafternoon heat & I see the sweat on her face, then the lines.

Don't forget, she says, pointing to the bag with the veggie burgers. *For him*.

Conversation with a Fantasy Mother

MARY JEAN CHAN

Dear fantasy mother, thank you
for taking my coming out as calmly
as a pond accepts a stone
flung into its depths.

You sieved my tears, added
an egg, then baked a beautiful cake.
You said: *Let us celebrate, for today*
you are reborn as my beloved.

The candles gleamed and the icing
was almost true – impossibly white –
coated with the sweetness of
sprinkles. We sat together

at the table and ate. Afterwards,
I returned to my room and touched
all the forbidden parts of myself, felt
a kindness I had not known in years.

Spalls

JANE CLARKE

To help us grow a garden, my mother and father travelled
across the Bog of Allen and over the Wicklow Gap.

They'd have preferred to drive west to Galway or Mayo,
they'd have preferred a husband and children

but their daughter loved a woman. We'd have the table set
for breakfast: rashers, black pudding, fried bread and eggs.

When the soil had warmed, we unloaded shovels
and rakes, buckets of compost and the rusted iron bar

for prising out rocks. The back seat was thronged
with pots of seedlings my mother had nurtured all winter.

We worked to her bidding: *loosen tangled roots before planting,*
sow marigolds next to beans, sprinkle Epsom salts around roses.

My father took off on his own to spud ragwort or clip a hedge.
One day he spent hours gathering stones of different shapes and sizes.

By evening he'd built us a wall under the holly, held together
by gravity and friction, hearted with handfuls of spalls.

At Fifty I Am Startled to Find I Am in My Splendor

SANDRA CISNEROS

These days I admit
I am wide as a *tule* tree.
My underwear protests.
And yet,

I like myself best
without clothes when
I can admire myself
as God made me, still
divine as a *maja*.
Wide as a fertility goddess,
though infertile. I am,
as they say,
in decline. Teeth
worn down, eyes burning
yellow. Of belly
bountiful and flesh
beneficent I am. I am
silvering in crags
of crotch and brow.
Amusing.

I am a spectator at my own sport.
I am Venetian, decaying splendidly.
Am magnificent beyond measure.
Lady Pompadour roses exploding

before death. Not old.
Correction, aged.
Passé? I am but vintage.

I am a woman of a delightful season.
El Cantarito, little brown jug of la Lotería.
Solid, stout, bottom planted
firmly and without a doubt,
filled to the brim I am.
I said the brim.

Homage to Li Po

DOUG ANDERSON

Woke up one morning to discover
I'd grown old. Last night's laughter,
ashes by the bed. Now,
my feet on the cold floor.
I get up to gather wood.
In the time it takes for the tea water to boil
I have replayed the movie of my life.
So much love clumsily spun like sunlight.
Where did it go?
I would have some of it back now.
But there is no wood, no tea.
And the fire comes from my heart.

Wrinkly Lady Dancer

ALICIA OSTRIKER

Going to be an old wrinkly lady
Going to be one of those frail rag people
Going to have withered hands and be
Puzzled to tears crossing the street

Hobble cautiously onto buses
Like a withery fruit
And quite silently sitting in this lurching bus
The avenues coming by

Some other passengers gaze at me
Clutching my cane and my newspaper
Seemingly protectively, but I will really be thinking about
The afternoon I danced naked with you
The afternoon I danced naked with you
The afternoon! I danced! Naked with you!

homage to my hips

LUCILLE CLIFTON

these hips are big hips
they need space to
move around in.
they don't fit into little
petty places. these hips
are free hips.
they don't like to be held back.
these hips have never been enslaved,
they go where they want to go
they do what they want to do.
these hips are mighty hips.
these hips are magic hips.
i have known them
to put a spell on a man and
spin him like a top!

When I Was at My Most Beautiful

NORIGO IBARAGI

translated from the Japanese by ANDREW HOUWEN *&* PETER ROBINSON

When I was at my most beautiful
towns came clattering down.
From most unexpected spots
the blue sky or suchlike I noticed.

When I was at my most beautiful
lots of people around me died
in factories, the sea, on nameless islands.
I did miss my chance to be well dressed.

When I was at my most beautiful
no one came with tender gifts.
Men only knew how to give a salute.
Merely pretty gazes they left as they set out.

When I was at my most beautiful
my head had nothing in it,
my heart had been hardened.
Only my arms and legs, chestnut-hued, shone.

When I was at my most beautiful
my homeland was overwhelmed by war.
Was there ever so stupid a thing?
Blouse sleeves rolled, I strode the humiliated town.

When I was at my most beautiful
jazz poured from the radio.
Dizzy, like smoking once more when you've stopped,
I devoured the exotic, sweet music.

When I was at my most beautiful
I was entirely unhappy,
I was completely incoherent,
I was absurdly lonely.

So I decided, if possible, I'd live a long life
like that French artist grandpa Rouault
who painted in old age outrageously fine pictures, wouldn't I?

Your Own Sensitivity at Least

NORIGO IBARAGI

translated from the Japanese
by ANDREW HOUWEN
& PETER ROBINSON

My brittle, parching heart,
don't blame it on the others.
Myself, I failed to water it.

Growing more difficult,
don't blame it on your friends.
Who was it lost the pliancy?

My own irritation,
don't blame it on the family.
I myself was bad at most things.

Early ardour nearly gone,
don't blame it on the daily round.
My spirit was enfeebled from the outset.

Each and every evil thing,
don't blame it on the times,
abandoned barely glinting self-esteem.

Your own sensitivity at least,
protect it by yourself,
you great idiot.

I Am Learning to Abandon the World

LINDA PASTAN

I am learning to abandon the world
before it can abandon me.
Already I have given up the moon
and snow, closing my shades
against the claims of white.
And the world has taken
my father, my friends.
I have given up melodic lines of hills,
moving to a flat, tuneless landscape.
And every night I give my body up
limb by limb, working upwards
across bone, towards the heart.
But morning comes with small
reprieves of coffee and birdsong.
A tree outside the window
which was simply shadow moments ago
takes back its branches twig
by leafy twig.
And as I take my body back
the sun lays its warm muzzle on my lap
as if to make amends.

I Am a Prayer

JOY HARJO

I am a prayer

I am a prayer of rain in the desert when the flowering ones
need a drink

I am a prayer

I am a prayer of sun when there is no end to night

I am a prayer

I am a prayer of ocean when there is no more blue

I am a prayer

I am a prayer of clouds when few make rain songs

I am a prayer

I am a prayer of roads that lead everywhere but home

I am a prayer

I am a prayer of white birds who cannot fly through a storm
of fear

I am a prayer

I am a prayer of fire who arrived to care for humans, then was
misused to destroy

I am a prayer

I am a prayer of wind, whose breathing carries seeds, pollen,
and songs to feed the generations

I am a prayer

I am a prayer of moon who wears the night as a shawl to hide
that which should never be spoken

I am a prayer

I am a prayer of grief, when life gambled with death and gave
up families for guns

I am a prayer

I am a prayer of smoke, wandering the broken houses, the littered
ground looking for a white flag of reason

I am a prayer

I am a prayer of mountains, those tall humble ones who agreed to
lift our eyes to see

I am a prayer

I am a prayer of forever making a path of beauty through the rubble
of eternity

I am a prayer

I am a prayer of poetry speaking the soundlessness of the dead who
return to speak in prayer

I am a prayer with children on my back roaming the earth house of
destruction and creation

I am a prayer without end

Carving

IMTIAZ DHARKER

Others can carve out
their space
in tombs and pyramids.
Our time cannot be trapped
in cages.
Nor hope, nor laughter.
We let the moment rise
like birds and planes and angels
to the sky.

Eternity is this.
Your breath on the window-pane,
living walls with shining eyes.
The surprise of spires,
uncompromising verticals. Knowing
we have been spared
to lift our faces up
for one more day,
into one more sunrise.

Flesh

KERRY HARDIE

Sitting in a doorway,
in October sunlight,
eating
peppers, onions, tomatoes,
stale bread sodden with olive oil –

and the air high and clean,
and the red taste of tomatoes,
and the sharp bite of onions,
and the pepper's scarlet crunch –

the body
coming awake again,
thinking,
maybe there's more to life than sickness,
than the body's craving for oblivion,
than the hunger of the spirit to be gone –

and maybe the body belongs in the world,
maybe it knows a thing or two,
maybe it's even possible
it may once more remember

sweetness,
absence of pain.

Suddenly Everything

ALYSON HALLETT

I've been watching clouds.
Sunday clouds above an estuary
stung with jet skis and sailing boats
with junk red sails. The speed
of them, the endless bleed of one
into the other.

'I never paid any attention
to clouds before,' the dying man says.

His fault then, that I'm lying here like this
looking at clouds as if they were the most
important things.

The idea behind the atmosphere.
The very things that guarantee life
on this tumbling bauble of rock.

Clouds bloom and dissolve
as the green hand of the wind
gardens their moist, white bodies
from one fantastic flower into the next.

No holding on up there.

The dying man is called Wolfgang.
'Every cloud outside my window,
every flower in the vase,
suddenly everything matters,' he says.

'i thank You God for most this amazing'

E.E. CUMMINGS

i thank You God for most this amazing
day:for the leaping greenly spirits of trees
and a blue true dream of sky;and for everything
which is natural which is infinite which is yes

(i who have died am alive again today,
and this is the sun's birthday;this is the birth
day of life and of love and wings:and of the gay
great happening illimitably earth)

how should tasting touching hearing seeing
breathing any—lifted from the no
of all nothing—human merely being
doubt unimaginable You?

(now the ears of my ears awake and
now the eyes of my eyes are opened)

Table

EDIP CANSEVER

translated from the Turkish
by JULIA CLAIRE TILLINGHAST
& RICHARD TILLINGHAST

A man filled with the gladness of living
Put his keys on the table,
Put flowers in a copper bowl there.
He put his eggs and milk on the table.
He put there the light that came in through the window,
Sound of a bicycle, sound of a spinning wheel.
The softness of bread and weather he put there.
On the table the man put
Things that happened in his mind.
What he wanted to do in life,
He put that there.
Those he loved, those he didn't love,
The man put them on the table too.
Three times three make nine:
The man put nine on the table.
He was next to the window next to the sky;
He reached out and placed on the table endlessness.
So many days he had wanted to drink a beer!
He put on the table the pouring of that beer.
He placed there his sleep and his wakefulness;
His hunger and his fullness he put there.

Now that's what I call a table!
It didn't complain at all about the load.
It wobbled once or twice, then stood firm.
The man kept piling things on.

'Set your course by the Sun...'

ELENA SHVARTS

translated from the Russian
by SASHA DUGDALE

Set your course by the Sun, the Sun
Although it has already slunk
Low to the marshy ground, the film-covered
Windows... And sunk.
But we may walk so light by the moon
The stars that play in the dusk
On a drum, as they move
Under the earth towards us.
In the single hour between sun and moon
Between star and choirs of stars
When the birds wait hushed,
For the conductor's words
Then I step out on the road,
Which leads neither South, nor North –
It leads to the dwellings of God
From where angels come forth
And hang like a rainbow
Over wicked bodily depths
And in this last moment of day
I manage a single step.

Living Space

IMTIAZ DHARKER

There are just not enough
straight lines. That
is the problem.
Nothing is flat
or parallel. Beams
balance crookedly on supports
thrust off the vertical.
Nails clutch at open seams.
The whole structure leans dangerously
towards the miraculous.

Into this rough frame,
someone has squeezed
a living space

and even dared to place
these eggs in a wire basket,
fragile curves of white
hung out over the dark edge
of a slanted universe,
gathering the light
into themselves,
as if they were
the bright, thin walls of faith.

Permission

BRENDAN KENNELLY

We lie here and know that peace
Is a raindrop on a blade of grass,
A globe of light inches from our eyes.

So our world retains its style
Of survival depending all the while
On what permits it to be complete and fragile.

Wake Up

ADAM ZAGAJEWSKI

translated from the Polish
by CLARE CAVANAGH

Wake up, my soul.
I don't know where you are,
where you're hiding,
but wake up, please,
we're still together,
the road is still before us,
a bright strip of dawn
will be our star.

Insha'Allah

DANUSHA LAMÉRIS

I don't know when it slipped into my speech
that soft word meaning, 'if God wills it'.
Insha'Allah I will see you next summer.
The baby will come in spring, insha'Allah.
Insha'Allah this year we will have enough rain.

So many plans I've laid have unraveled
easily as braids beneath my mother's quick fingers.

Every language must have a word for this. A word
our grandmothers uttered under their breath
as they pinned the whites, soaked in lemon,
hung them to dry in the sun, or peeled potatoes,
dropping the discarded skins into a bowl.

Our sons will return next month, insha'Allah.
Insha'Allah this war will end, soon. Insha'Allah
the rice will be enough to last through winter.

How lightly we learn to hold hope,
as if it were an animal that could turn around
and bite your hand. And still we carry it
the way a mother would, carefully,
from one day to the next.

The door

MIROSLAV HOLUB

translated from the Czech
by IAN MILNER

Go and open the door.
   Maybe outside there's
   a tree, or a wood,
   a garden,
   or a magic city.

Go and open the door.
   Maybe a dog's rummaging.
   Maybe you'll see a face,
or an eye,
or the picture
         of a picture.

Go and open the door.
   If there's a fog
   it will clear.

Go and open the door.
   Even if there's only
   the darkness ticking,
   even if there's only
   the hollow wind,
   even if
      nothing
         is there,
go and open the door.

                 At least
                 there'll be
                 a draught.

A Portable Pardise

ROGER ROBINSON

And if I speak of Paradise,
then I'm speaking of my grandmother
who told me to carry it always
on my person, concealed, so
no one else would know but me.
That way they can't steal it, she'd say.
And if life puts you under pressure,
trace its ridges in your pocket,
smell its piney scent on your handkerchief,
hum its anthem under your breath.
And if your stresses are sustained and daily,
get yourself to an empty room – be it hotel,
hostel or hovel – find a lamp
and empty your paradise onto a desk:
your white sands, green hills and fresh fish.
Shine the lamp on it like the fresh hope
of morning, and keep staring at it till you sleep.

Decisions: II

BORIS A. NOVAK

translated from the Slovenian
by MIA DINTINJANA

Between two words
choose the quieter one.

Between word and silence
choose listening.

Between two books
choose the dustier one.

Between the earth and the sky
choose a bird.

Between two animals
choose the one who needs you more.

Between two children
choose both.

Between the lesser and the bigger evil
choose neither.

Between hope and despair
choose hope:
it will be harder to bear.

The Spaces of Hope

IVAN V. LALIĆ

translated from the Serbian
by FRANCIS R. JONES

I have experienced the spaces of hope,
The spaces of a moderate mercy. Experienced
The places which suddenly set
Into a random form: a lilac garden,
A street in Florence, a morning room,
A sea smeared with silver before the storm,
Or a starless night lit only
By a book on the table. The spaces of hope
Are in time, not linked into
A system of miracles, nor into a unity;
They merely exist. As in Kanfanar,
At the station; wind in a wild vine
A quarter-century ago: one space of hope.

Another, set somewhere in the future,
Is already destroying the void around it,
Unclear but real. Probable.

In the spaces of hope light grows,
Free of charge, and voices are clearer,
Death has a beautiful shadow, the lilac blooms later,
But for that it looks like its first-ever flower.

Hope

LISEL MUELLER

It hovers in dark corners
before the lights are turned on,
it shakes sleep from its eyes
and drops from mushroom gills,
it explodes in the starry heads
of dandelions turned sages,
it sticks to the wings of green angels
that sail from the tops of maples.
It sprouts in each occluded eye
of the many-eyed potato,
it lives in each earthworm segment
surviving cruelty,
it is the motion that runs the tail of a dog,
it is the mouth that inflates the lungs
of the child that has just been born.
It is the singular gift
we cannot destroy in ourselves,
the argument that refutes death,
the genius that invents the future,
all we know of God.
It is the serum which makes us swear
not to betray one another;
it is in this poem, trying to speak.

Hope

ENDA COYLE-GREENE

She has a sense of somewhere beyond
here where there is hope. A note cools
on a piano in a room long emptied,
and so well that only the ghosts notice.
She is aware of them all; they catch her
breathing now and then, attempting to
turn around again in a space that grows
narrow but not bitter with age:
the nights end-stage perhaps, its black edge
stopped dead by a sliver of morning light;
the certainty of sorts of a day
where something, anything, might happen.
Oscillating, she assumes the shape, skin-
slipping to a place where she can wait.

Hope

EDITH SÖDERGRAN

translated from the Finland Swedish
by DAVID McDUFF

I want to be unconstrained –
therefore I care not a fig for noble styles.
I roll up my sleeves.
The poem's dough is rising…
Oh what a pity
that I cannot bake cathedrals…
Highness of forms –
goal of persistent longing.
Child of the present –
does your spirit not have a proper shell?
Before I die
I shall bake a cathedral.

Hope

ELLEN CRANITCH

Look out at dusk to the west of Bcharre,
from the small basilica with its red-tiled tower.
All is hushed around you. Mist on the vineyards.
Smoke rising from a few houses below.
A dog's bark rings out across the gorge
and the great hollows of air, slung across,
catch the rebounding sound. The opening hills
are hands that waft you. There is so much hope
in the view. I would wish to be ushered
by the Qadisha valley which the cedars
of Lebanon call home: though it's the sunset,
the day's end, you gaze at, to all who are
harboured by this sacred landscape
its breath is refuge, its face is dawn.

The Lamp

AI QING

translated from the Chinese
by ROBERT DORSETT

Hope that looked toward the horizon
now lies in this oil lamp –
For the sky's farther than hope can reach!
Arrows of light obliterate the distance
into blank nothingness;
then what makes my trembling fingers
gently stroke the brilliant forehead
of this oil lamp?

[1933–1935, in prison]

Now

SAMUEL MENASHE

There is never an end to loss, or hope
I give up the ghost for which I grope
Over and over again saying *Amen*
To all that does or does not happen –
The eternal event is now, not when

Dreams

LANGSTON HUGHES

Hold fast to dreams
For if dreams die
Life is a broken-winged bird
That cannot fly.

Hold fast to dreams
For when dreams go
Life is a barren field
Frozen with snow.

Harlem [2]

LANGSTON HUGHES

What happens to a dream deferred?

Does it dry up
like a raisin in the sun?
Or fester like a sore –
And then run?
Does it stink like rotten meat?
Or crust and sugar over –
like a syrupy sweet?

Maybe it just sags
like a heavy load.

Or does it explode?

Good Souls, to Survive

BRENDAN KENNELLY

Things inside things endure
Longer than things exposed;
We see because we are blind
And should not be surprised to find
We survive because we're enclosed.

If merit is measured at all,
Vulnerability is the measure;
The little desire protection
With something approaching passion,
Will not be injured, cannot face error.

So the bird in astonishing flight
Chokes on the stricken blood,
The bull in the dust is one
With surrendered flesh and bone,
Naked on chill wood.

The real is rightly intolerable,
Its countenance stark and abrupt,
Good souls, to survive, select
Their symbols from among the elect –
Articulate, suave, corrupt.

But from corruption comes the deep
Desire to plunge to the true;
To dare is to redeem the blood,
Discover the buried good,
Be vulnerably new.

Against Panic

MOLLY FISK

You recall those times, I know you do, when the sun
lifted its weight over a small rise to warm your face,
when a parched day finally broke open, real rain
sluicing down the sidewalk, rattling city maples
and you so sure the end was here, life a house of cards
tipped over, falling, hope's last breath extinguished
in a bitter wind. Oh, friend, search your memory again –
beauty and relief are still there, only sleeping.

The Well 2

MICHAEL D. HIGGINS

To visit again the well of friendship,
And draw on the end of an old rope
The bucket of one's life,
To listen as it clatters
Against the sides,
Making a rattling resonance of childhood,
Is the stuff of pilgrimage.
To make the long haul back
For a sweet drink
From a decrepit vessel
Binds up time.
Water hidden under the earth emerges
And makes a renewal.
The deep drink forges an old unity
Beyond all uncertainty.

A Healing

LEANNE O'SULLIVAN

That first day of springtime thaw when the ice
began to melt and pour down the mountains,
I walked to the top of the old mining road
to hear all the slow loosening and letting go;
the kick-back of copper and clay from my heels,
the steady blasts following like the sound
of another person's footfall on the shale,
spirited behind me; the streams that thundered
down to disappear again underground
so the whole place was all tremble and go,
lightening into a stiller and clearer air.
I loved the copper-lit, the downhill skid and slack,
the water roaring out of time, turning back
with so much sound and rush that it seemed
to be gathering strength from ore and dust and clay,
under the shade of that green and beaten ground.

Seed

PAULA MEEHAN

The first warm day of spring
and I step out into the garden from the gloom
of a house where hope had died
to tally the storm damage, to seek what may
have survived. And finding some forgotten
lupins I'd sown from seed last autumn
holding in their fingers a raindrop each
like a peace offering, or a promise,
I am suddenly grateful and would
offer a prayer if I believed in God.
But not believing, I bless the power of seed,
its casual, useful persistence,
and bless the power of sun,
its conspiracy with the underground,
and thank my stars the winter's ended.

Everything Is Going To Be All Right

DEREK MAHON

How should I not be glad to contemplate
the clouds clearing beyond the dormer window
and a high tide reflected on the ceiling?
There will be dying, there will be dying,
but there is no need to go into that.
The lines flow from the hand unbidden
and the hidden source is the watchful heart;
the sun rises in spite of everything
and the far cities are beautiful and bright.
I lie here in a riot of sunlight
watching the day break and the clouds flying.
Everything is going to be all right.

NOTES ON THE POETS

Doug Anderson (*b.* 1943) served in Vietnam as a corpsman with a US Marine infantry battalion in 1967. His books include *Keep Your Head Down: Vietnam, the Sixties, and a Journey of Self-Discovery* (2009), and poetry collections including *The Moon Reflected Fire* (1994). He has taught at colleges including the William Joiner Center for the Study of War and Its Social Consequences, and latterly at Emerson College, Boston.

Mona Arshi is a poet, novelist and essayist, born in London of Sikh Punjabi heritage. She worked as a human rights lawyer at Liberty before starting to write poetry, completing her Masters in poetry in 2011 at the University of East Anglia. Her debut collection *Small Hands* (Pavilion) won the Forward Prize for Best First Collection in 2015, and was followed by *Dear Big Gods* in 2019. Her poems are notable for their lightness of touch, with a delicacy that belies their force, whether the subject is pain, violence, grief or hope for the world, for the earth's tiny creatures and its 'churning, broken song'.

Stanisłav Barańczak (1946-2014) was a leading Polish poet, critic and translator (notably of Wisława Szymborska) who engaged with the politics of Eastern Europe in all his writing, which was banned during Poland's most repressive years. His poetry was both playful and formally inventive in addressing his main theme: the fundamental injustice, shame and horror of the human condition. In his view, 'writing poetry is perhaps nothing more than trying to play a straight man to that rambling, rambunctious, never-to-be-interrupted, always-on-a-roll, stand-up comic, the world'.

Ellen Bass (*b.* 1947) is a leading American poet also known as co-author of the controversial bestseller, *The Courage to Heal* (1981), written during two decades of working with survivors of childhood sexual abuse. She studied with Anne Sexton at Boston University, and has published nine poetry collections, most recently *Indigo* (2020) and *Like a Beggar* (2014), which 'pulses with sex, humour and compassion', according to the *New York Times*. These recur in her poetry because, she says, 'we are all so terribly imperfect – starting with myself. And that willingness to feel, even a little, what someone else is feeling is what joins us most intimately to others.'

Jorge Luis Borges (1899–1986) is best known for his philosophical short fiction exploring dreams, labyrinths, mirrors and myths, but started publishing his poetry earlier than his prose. Following the publication of his debut collection in 1923, he continued to compose poetry – on similar themes to his prose – throughout his life, devoting more time to poems he could memorise as his eyesight deteriorated, becoming completely blind by age of 55.

Born in Buenos Aires, he grew up speaking both Spanish and English. As a child he'd thought at first that English was the language of the top part of the large family house where his English grandmother Fanny lived. But his father also spoke English, and Borges referred to his father's English library of hundreds of books as the chief event in his life. He was also an obsessive translator of English, French and German literature, and especially enjoyed translating Anglo-Saxon and Old Norse poetry into Spanish, and could recite much or all of *Beowulf* from memory after he'd lost his sight.

Lucie Brock-Boido (1956–2018) was an American poet known for her sensual, inventive and gorgeous-sounding poetry, which she herself called 'feral'. Influenced primarily by Wallace Stevens but also by Emily Dickinson, she published four collections, the last being *Stay, Illusion* in 2013, when she told *Guernica* magazine: 'I came to poetry because I felt I couldn't live properly in the real world.' *Soul Keeping Company* (2010), a selection from her first three books, was published by Carcanet in the UK.

Jericho Brown (*b.* 1976) is an African American poet from Louisiana who worked at one time as a speech writer for the Mayor of Orleans and is now a professor at Emory University. He has published three collections, exploring themes such as fatherhood, legacy, blackness, queerness, the body and trauma with explosive power and formal virtuosity. His invention of the duplex – a combination of the sonnet, the ghazal and the blues – is testament to his impressive formal skill.

Edip Cansever (1928–86) was one of Turkey's leading post-war poets. He went from school into business at his father's antiques shop in Istanbul, later lamenting that he hadn't studied philosophy. First published in 1954 in his second book of poems, 'Table' became a talismanic poem for Turkish readers but was a mixed blessing for its author: he said if he had written nothing other than this poem, 'it would have been worth it. And yet I haven't been able to escape from this poem ever in my life.'

Giorgio Caproni (1912–90) was an Italian poet whose work was fundamentally changed by the Second World War, when he worked as a school teacher while also being active in the Italian Resistance. His collection *The Passage of Aeneas* (1956) is notable for its existential examination of the effects of war. This was followed by *The Seed of Crying* (1959), poems remembering his mother Anna Picchi and his childhood in Livorno. The landscapes, light, air, weather, earth, soil and rocks of his native Liguria exert a strong presence in his poetry which is both naturalistic and metaphorical.

Mary Jean Chan (*b*. 1990) is a Hong Kong-Chinese poet, lecturer, editor and critic whose debut poetry collection, *Flèche*, won the 2019 Costa Poetry Award, and was followed by *Bright Fear* in 2023. Their French title *Flèche* relates to Chan's prowess as a fencer during their school years, pointing to the intertwined themes of their poetry: skin, race, identity, queerness, multilingualism and postcolonial legacy. Chan now lives and teaches in the UK.

Chen Chen was born in 1989 in Xiamen, China, and 'grew up' in Massachusetts in the US. He has published two collections, *When I Grow Up I Want to Be a List of Further Possibilities* (2017 US; 2019 UK) and *Your Emergency Contact Has Experienced an Emergency* (2022). His idiosyncratic poems are both zany and heartbreaking, exploring family – blood and chosen – and examining what one inherits and what one invents, as a queer Asian American living through an era of Trump, mass shootings and the Covid-19 pandemic.

Julius Chingono (1946–2011) was born in Norton, Zimbabwe, the son of a farmworker, and worked for most of his life as a blaster in the mines. Made redundant in 1999, he worked intermittently as a rock-blasting contractor. His poem 'As I Go' depicts a life stripped to its essentials. 'His often deceptively simple poetry was written with compassion and clarity, feeling deeply as he did for the hardships of the poor and marginalised, while his honesty, humour and ironic eye made him a sharp and witty observer of those who abused their station through corruption and hypocrisy.' [*Poetry International Web*]

Sandra Cisneros was born in Chicago in 1954 to a family of Mexican heritage who were constantly moving between the US and Mexico. The early success of her novel *The House on Mango Street* (1983) led to her becoming the first Chicana writer to have her books published by a mainstream publisher. Much of her work work deals with poverty, misogyny, Chicana identity and the challenges of being caught between Mexican and Anglo-American cultures. She has received wide recognition for her poetry as well as for her novels and short stories.

Jane Clarke (*b.* 1961) grew up on a farm in Co. Roscommon. Rooted in Irish rural life, this poet of poignant observation achieves restraint and containment while communicating intense emotions, bearing witness to the rhythms of birth and death, celebration and mourning, endurance and regrowth. After working for many years in psychoanalytic psychotherapy, she took an MPhil in Writing from the University of South Wales, and went on to publish three highly praised collections, *The River* (2015), *When the Tree Falls* (2019) and *A Change in the Air* (2023).

Lucille Clifton (1936–2010) was a prolific African American poet, writer and educator from Buffalo. Her work emphasises endurance and strength through adversity, particularly in African-American communities. The first poet to have two books chosen as finalists for the Pulitzer Prize, she later received the Ruth Lilly Poetry Prize in 2007, with the judges commenting: 'One always feels the looming humaneness around Lucille Clifton's poems – it is a moral quality that some poets have and some don't.' Asked how she'd like to be remembered, she said: 'I would like to be seen as a woman whose roots go back to Africa, who tried to honor being human. My inclination is to try to help.'

Born in London of Irish parents, **Ellen Cranitch** is a poet, lecturer and journalist. She has published two collections, most recently *Crystal* (2024), which traces the arc of a woman's experience after discovering that her partner is addicted to crystal meth. Her poem 'Hope' appears towards the end of that book, from a place of healing. In a poem preceding it called 'Beauty', she writes of 'the power of beauty /

that it is grounded in our capacity to feel pity, to feel grief', and how it is 'to feel connected, to life, to others […] It is what steps in to offer you connection when you are most alone.'

Enda Coyle-Greene (*b.* 1954) divided her formative years between Dublin's iconic Moore Street and Rathfarnham. Her many and varied jobs included a long stint in international freight forwarding before deciding to take her poetry seriously. After graduating from the Seamus Heaney Centre for Poetry at Queen's University, Belfast, she won the Patrick Kavanagh Award for her debut collection, *Snow Negatives* (2007), and has since published two further collections, *Map of the Last* (2013) and *Indigo, Electric, Baby* (2020). She is Artistic Director of the Fingal Poetry Festival which she co-founded.

Lorna Crozier (*b.* 1948) is one of Canada's most loved poets. Born in Swift Current, Saskatchewan, she grew up in a prairie community where the local heroes were hockey players and curlers, and 'never once thought of being a writer'. While working as a high school English teacher she had a poem taken by a magazine which turned her life towards writing. She has published 16 books of poetry, a memoir and non-fiction titles. Whether writing about angels, ageing, or Louis Armstrong's trout sandwich, she continues to engage readers and writers across Canada and the world with her grace, wisdom and wit.

Edward Estlin Cummings (1894–1962) was born in Cambridge, Massachusetts, the son of a Unitarian minister. Like his parents, his religious beliefs were influenced by the New England Transcendentalists. He grew up knowing many family friends from that cultural and intellectual milieu, including the philosopher William James. E.E. Cummings was a prolific as well as a popular poet, the author of 12 volumes of highly distinctive, often eccentric poetry, arguing in the introduction to his fourth collection, *is 5* (1926), that poetry should be viewed not as a 'product' but a 'process'. It was his publishers, not Cummings himself, who began printing his name all in lower case, playing upon the subversion of typographical convention in his poetry, and this came to be how his name was printed in anthologies, but in recent years his estate has insisted that publishers print his name with capital letters, as we have done here.

Imtiaz Dharker (*b.* 1954) grew up 'a Muslim Calvinist' in a Lahori household in Glasgow, was adopted by India, and now lives in London. She is a poet, artist and video filmmaker, and all her poetry collections are illustrated with her drawings, which form an integral part of her books; she is one of very few poet-artists to work in this way. She received The Queen's Gold Medal for Poetry for 2014 from H.M. Queen Elizabeth, and in 2019 was appointed Chancellor of Newcastle University. Her main themes are drawn from a life of transitions: childhood, exile, journeying, home, displacement, religious strife and terror, and latterly, grief.

Little-known outside America, **Jack Gilbert** (1925-2012) was a latterday metaphysical poet whose work replays the myth of Orpheus and Eurydice, recurrent figures in his books. Born in Pittsburgh, he spent much of his adult life in Greece, mostly on the island of Paros. His poetry bears witness to what he called 'the craft of the invisible', that is, form in the service of his explosive content. James Dickey called him 'a necessary poet': 'He takes himself away to a place more inward than it is safe to go; from that awful silence and tightening, he returns to us poems of savage compassion.'

Lauren Haldeman is an American poet and graphic artist who has published three poetry collections and a graphic novel, *Team Photograph* (2022). Her second collection, *Instead of Dying* (2017), probes the world of death with a powerful mix of humour, epiphany and agonising grief, imagining alternative realities for a lost brother and relentlessly recording the unlived possibilities that blossom from the purgative magical thinking of mourning. She works as a web developer and editor.

Originally from Somerset, **Alyson Hallett** is a poet who has worked on many collaborations with dancers, musicians, scientists, visual artists and sculptors, with a particular interest in having poems embedded in public places. In 2001 she began working on *The Migration Habits of Stones*, a continuing poetry and public art project that involves journeying around the world with a stone, looking at migration, displacement, and how we make kin with stones and rocks.

Kerry Hardie (*b.* 1951) is an Irish writer who has published ten books of poetry and two novels. Often following the annual round of rural life, her poetry questions, celebrates and challenges all aspects of life and experience, exploring the mystery of 'why we are here', but is ultimately concerned with the quiet realisation that 'there is nothing to do in the world except live in it'. A number of her poems are narratives or parables in which experience yields a spiritual lesson and consolation; others chart a coming to terms with death or continuing illness and an acceptance of inevitability or flux.

Joy Harjo (*b*. 1951) is a Native American poet and storyteller who in 2019 became the first Native American to be appointed US Poet Laureate, serving for three terms. Her signature project was *Living Nations, Living Words: A Map of First Peoples Poetry*. Influenced by her own Muscogee Nation traditions, her work is grounded in her relationship with the earth on a physical, spiritual and mythopoetic level. She is also a multi-talented performer and saxophonist, combining poetry and chanting with tribal music, jazz, funk and rock.

Michael D. Higgins (*b*. 1941) has served as the ninth President of Ireland since 2011. He was previously Mayor of Galway, Ireland's minister for arts, culture and the Gaeltacht, and president of the Labour Party. He has published five books of poetry, and has often included poems – in Irish and English – in his speeches.

Edward Hirsch (*b*. 1950) is a Chicago-born American poet who has published nine collections of his own poetry but has written even more about the work of other poets. His most popular book has been *How to Read a Poem and Fall in Love with Poetry* (1999). The trademarks of his poems, according to Jhumpa Lahiri, are 'to be intimate but restrained, to be tender without being sentimental, to witness life without flinching, and above all, to isolate and preserve those details of our existence so often overlooked, so easily forgotten, so essential to our souls.'

Jack Hirschman (1933–2021) was a prolific American poet and social activist, known for his radical engagement with both poetry and politics, working 'for the Communist movement for 45 years, and the new class of impoverished and homeless people'. Born in New York City of Russian Jewish parentage, he lived in California for much of his life, already the long-time Whitmanesque poet of the streets and people of San Francisco when he was made the city's Poet Laureate in 2006. He forged strong connections with leftist writers in Europe, translating many poets from several languages, and identifying with Mayakovsky ('the first street poet of the century') in particular.

Jane Hirshfield (*b*. 1953) is a visionary American poet who trained as a Zen Buddhist. Born in New York City, she has lived in northern California since 1974, for over 30 years in a small white cottage looking out on fruit trees, old roses and Mt Tamalpais. Her poems are both sensual meditations and passionate investigations which reveal complex truths in language luminous and precise. Rooted in the living world, they celebrate and elucidate a hard-won affirmation of our human fate. Her retrospective, *The Asking*, was published in 2024.

Miroslav Holub (1923–98) was Czechoslovakia's foremost modern poet, and one of her leading immunologists, but suffered from censorship during the Soviet period. Often employing scientific metaphors, his fantastical and witty poems give a scientist's bemused view of human folly and other life on the planet. Mixing myth, history and folktale with science and philosophy, his plainly written, sceptical poems are surreal mini-dramas often pivoting on paradoxes.

Alfred Edward Housman (1859–1936) was a brilliant classical scholar who became a highly popular poet some years after the publication of his collection, *A Shropshire Lad*, in 1896. George Orwell attributed the book's popularity with Edwardian youth and with young soldiers in particular to its nostalgia for the countryside; its pessimistic 'adolescent' themes of murder, suicide, unhappy love and doomed or early death; and its 'bitter, defiant paganism, a conviction that life is short and the gods are against you, which exactly fitted the prevailing mood of the young'. Death is part of nature in a hostile universe abandoned by God, while youthful beauty is cherished for only as long as it lasts. Its author's unrequited homosexual leanings are barely disguised but were largely responsible for his later collection, *More Poems*, not being published until after his death, in 1936. Our untitled poem is taken from that volume.

Marie Howe (*b*. 1950) is one of America's most daring and courageous poets. She has published four collections over three decades, with a retrospective, *What the Earth Seemed to Say*, out in 2024. Her poetry explores the themes of relationship, attachment and loss in a personal search for transcendence. With its 'radical simplicity and seriousness of purpose, along with a fearless interest in autobiography and its tragedies and redemptions' (Matthew Zapruder), it transforms penetrating observations of everyday life into sacred, humane miracles.

Langston Hughes (1902–67) was a central figure in the Harlem Renaissance of the 1920s, known for his vivid portrayals of Black life in America as well as for his engagement with the world of jazz. He published his debut collection, *The Weary Blues*, in 1926, and became the first African-American to make a living from writing. His pioneering efforts brought Black literature and music to national attention, undoubtedly opening the way for a subsequent generation of Black writers.

The syncopated rhythms of his 'jazz poetry' were absorbed even further afield: not only in the US by the Beats and the East and West Coast writers of the 50s, but in Britain, in the work of Christopher Logue, Michael Horovitz, Alexander Trocchi, Adrian Mitchell and others. For some, Hughes's writing was not militant enough (he sought 'change through the force of his art'), but his hymns to civil rights remain some of the most moving and memorable ever written, including his Whitmanesque 'I, too, sing America'. He founded Black theatre groups in Harlem, Chicago and Los Angeles, and maintained a prolific output of books, publishing poetry, short stories and cultural history, as well as two autobiographies and a *Selected Poems* (1959).

Noriko Ibaragi (1926–2006) was a Japanese poet who began publishing poetry at a time when published women poets were a rarity, and helped to pave the way for countless Japanese women poets. Her poetry's combination of lyrical beauty, political awareness and a refreshing directness has been influential across post-war Japanese poetry. As she would later lament in her famous 1957 poem 'When I Was at My Most Beautiful' (set to music by Pete Seeger), Japan had been at war throughout most of her teenage years, from the time she started junior high school to the end of her teens. 'Your Own Sensitivity at Least' from 1977 expresses a frankness and 'free rein' for the individual in keeping with a time of social and economic liberation for Japanese women. The poem affirms the power of the individual not to blame or rely on others, but to shape their own destiny and resist being reduced by experience to cowardly excuses. Its boldness remains equally powerful and subversive in today's Japan. [*Thanks to translator Andrew Houwen for this summary.*]

Jeong Ho-seung (*b.* 1950) is probably Korea's most popular poet. His delicately nuanced treatment of such vital themes as desire, love, beauty, time, pain, loss and death has long made him a favourite among readers, according to his translators Brother Anthony of Taizé and Susan Hwang. 'The wisdom embodied in the collected poems [of Jeong] is universal in its scope, leading readers toward an awareness of the metaphysical, invisible dimensions of human existence, where faith is rooted.' Jeong himself has his own theory: 'Everyone is a poet. Yet some people write poetry, while others do not... I am writing the poems that other people should have written, instead of them. Readers will be able to find their own lives in these poems.'

Vincent Katz (*b.* 1960) is an American poet, translator, critic, editor, art writer, collaborator and curator, the author of 14 books of poetry, most recently *Broadway for Paul* (2020), and his award-winning translation, *The Complete Elegies of Sextus Propertius* (2004). The subway focus of his poem 'This Beautiful Bubble' is typical of a poet of whom critics have written: 'Vincent's commitment to motion is optimistic and true hearted. These poems approach the city from inside and out, bringing to light the fact that the whole world is a container of networks.' [1992] 'Katz's poetry offers Lower East Side visions of travel throughout the world, treating the everyday with characteristic enthusiasm, beatific charm – and occasional absurdist humour.' [1994]

Brendan Kennelly (1936–2021) was a hugely popular Irish poet, critic and dramatist who taught at Trinity College Dublin for over 30 years. He grew up in the village of Ballylongford in Co. Kerry, and most of his work is concerned with the people, landscapes, wildlife and history of Ireland, and with language, religion and politics. Best-known for three controversial poetry books, *Cromwell* (1983), *The Book of Judas* (1991) and *Poetry My Arse* (1995), he was a much loved public figure in Ireland, and a popular guest on television programmes. His poem 'Begin' (included in *Soul Food*) was widely circulated by Irish Americans in the aftermath of 9/11.

John Koethe (*b.* 1945) is an American poet and

philosopher with a particular interest, in both roles, in the philosophy of language. According to the critic Robert Hahn, 'Koethe's poetry is ultimately lyrical, and its claim on us comes not from philosophy's dream of precision but from the common human dream that our lives make some kind of sense. What Koethe offers is not ideas but a weave of reflection, emotion, and music; what he creates is art – a bleak, harrowing art in all it chooses to confront, but one whose rituals and repetitions contain the hope of renewal.' In his most recent collection, *Beyond Belief* (2022) Koethe poses essential questions about the rhythms of time, language and literature, and the meaning of life.

Arun Kolatkar (1931–2004) was one of India's greatest modern poets. He wrote prolifically, in both Marathi and English, but did not publish a book of poems until he was 44. His poetry offers a rich description of India while at the same time performing a complex act of devotion, discovering the divine trace in a degenerate world. Jeet Thayil attributed its popularity in India to 'the Kolatkarean voice: unhurried, lit with whimsy, unpretentious even when making learned literary or mythological allusions. And whatever the poet's eye alights on – particularly the odd, the misshapen, and the famished – receives the gift of close attention.'

Ted Kooser (*b*. 1939) is an American poet and essayist whose work celebrates a vanishing way of life, with a focus on people and places in Nebraska and the Midwest. Common themes of his thoughtful, conversational poetry include love, family and the passage of time. After working for many years in the life insurance business, he retired in 1999 as a vice president. He served as the 13th US Poet Laureate from 2004 to 2006, founding *American Life in Poetry*, a service offering a free weekly poem to newspapers across the US, aimed at raising the public visibility of poetry. His collection *Delights & Shadows* won the 2005 Pulitzer Prize for poetry. Kooser has commented: 'I write for other people with the hope that I can help them to see the wonderful things within their everyday experiences. In short, I want to show people how interesting the ordinary world can be if you pay attention.'

Lal Ded (Mother Lalla or Lalleshwari) was a 14th-century mystic seer, the first in a long list of saints preaching the medieval mysticism which spread throughout India. Married at 12, she later escaped her husband and abusive mother-in-law to become a wandering ascetic, singing of her bliss and love for the Divine, her followers including Hindus as well as Muslims. The Kashmiri language is full of her many wise sayings.

Ivan V. Lalić (1931–96) was a major figure in European poetry. Born in Belgrade, a Yugoslav poet who was to become a Serbian poet, he lived through traumatic times, witnessing the deaths of school friends in an air raid and dying as his homeland was wracked by ethnic division. His poetry is marked by the knowledge of sudden, brutal death and the profound sense of responsibility entailed by survival: a duty to remember, to bear witness and to face the crucial questions of human existence.

Danusha Laméris is a poet and an essayist who was born in Cambridge, Massachusetts in 1971 to a Dutch father and a Barbadian mother and raised in Northern California. She has published two collections, with a third forthcoming from Copper Canyon Press. Each of her poems offers a compelling, slow-revealing human story, with themes including motherhood, community, desire, sorrow, beauty, the body and death.

Denise Levertov (1923–97), one of the 20th century's foremost American poets, was born in England, the daughter of a Russian Jewish scholar turned Anglican priest and a Welsh Congregationalist mother, both parents descended from mystics. She sent her poems as a child to T.S. Eliot, who admired and encouraged her. In 1948, she emigrated to America. Susan J. Zeuenbergen wrote of her work: 'Meditative and evocative, Levertov's poetry concerns itself with the search for meaning. She sees the poet's role as a priestly one; the poet is the mediator between ordinary people and the divine mysteries.' Throughout her life, Denise Levertov worked also as a political activist, campaigning tirelessly for civil rights and environmental causes, and against the Vietnam War, the Bomb and US-backed regimes in Latin America.

Ada Limón (*b.* 1976) is a poet of Mexican-American descent who in 2022 became the first Latina to be appointed US Poet Laureate, picked for being 'a poet who connects' whose 'accessible, engaging poems ground us in where we are and who we share the world with. They speak of intimate truths, of the beauty and heartbreak that is living, in ways that help us move forward.' Her signature project is *You Are Here* which focuses on how poetry can help connect us to the natural world. In 2023 she unveiled her NASA-commissioned poem 'In Praise of Mystery' which connects two water worlds, Earth and Jupiter's moon Europa, to be engraved on a plaque carried aboard the Europa Clipper spacecraft, set to launch in October 2024 on its voyage to Jupiter and its moons.

Adriana Lisboa (*b.* 1970) is a Brazilian writer known for her poetry, fiction and books for children. A former musician and music teacher, she trained in Zen meditation. Her interest in Japanese classical poetry and culture – and the poetry of Basho in particular – led to her studying Japanese during a fellowship in Kyoto. In a 2015 interview with *Words Without Borders* she described how her Buddhist practice and studies – latterly in the Tibetan tradition – have had a deep impact on the way she lives and works: 'Concepts like the emptiness and no-self of all things that can sound really difficult to grasp from an intellectual point of view, open themselves up to you through the practice of meditation, and really become a new way of perceiving things. All is really contingent and mostly unpredictable – we all know

that, of course, but we don't live accordingly. These are notions that I like to explore in my prose and my poetry, as well as a sort of unbiased empathy for my characters, whoever they are.'

John McCullough (*b.* 1978) is an English poet whose main influences have been the work of American writers such as Frank O'Hara, August Kleinzahler and Elizabeth Bishop as well as the Anglo-American Thom Gunn. Sharing their commitment to finding new, exciting means of expression has been essential in John McCullough's exploration of 21st-century queer life in England. There is often a sense of wonder and delight in the universe in his playful poetry, 'a sense that life can be perpetually strange and fascinating; that we're always on the edge of something new' (Catherine Smith).

Kona Macphee was born in London in 1969 and grew up in Australia, where she studied musical composition at the Sydney Conservatorium, violin at the University of Sydney, and computer science and robotics at Monash University. She has worked as a software designer and motorcycle mechanic. Based for many years now in Scotland, she has published three collections, including *Perfect Blue* (2010), winner of the Geoffrey Faber Memorial Prize, from which her poem 'The gift' was taken.

Sandra McPherson (*b.* 1943) is an American poet who writes of relationships with family and friends with intimacy as well as restraint. Each of her collections bears witness to key events in her life: marriage, motherhood, divorce, a daughter's autism, remarriage, relations with adoptive parents, and a midlife reunion with birth parents, but with a visionary perspective rooted in everyday experience.

Derek Mahon (1941–2020) was the most formally accomplished Irish poet of a generation including Seamus Heaney and Michael Longley. Born in Belfast, the son of a shipyard worker, he studied French and English at Trinity College Dublin. Living in France and other countries for some years, he explored themes of isolation, aloneness and alienation in his poetry His early influences included classical literature, Yeats, MacNeice and Beckett along with the French Symbolist poets he continued to translate, along with the poetry of Philippe Jaccottet.

Born in Catalonia, **Joan Margarit** (1938–2021) was an architect as well as a poet and translator, and from 1968 until his retirement was a Professor at Barcelona's Technical School of Architecture, working for part of that time on Gaudí's Sagrada Família cathedral. The melancholy and candour of his poetry show his affinity with Thomas Hardy, whose work he translated. He first published poetry in Spanish, but after four books decided to write in Catalan. From 1980 he began to establish his reputation as a major Catalan poet. In *Tugs in the Fog: Selected Poems* (2006), Joan Margarit evoked the Spanish Civil War and its aftermath, the harshness of life in Barcelona under Franco, and grief at the death of a beloved handicapped daughter, reminding us that it is not death we have to understand but life.

Irish poet and playwright **Paula Meehan** was born in 1955 in north Dublin, growing up in a working-class community which made her acutely aware of urban poverty. She studied at Trinity College Dublin, and at Eastern Washington University in the US, spending time with poet-professors Gary Snyder and Carolyn Kizer during a formative period for her poetry. Back in Dublin she started holding writing workshops for prisoners and low-income communities in inner-city Dublin at the same time as her early collections were published. Her poetry is known for its wit, craft and power, for its wide range, and for focussing on the minutiae of people's lives enlivened by an awareness of the politics of gender and class. She was Ireland Professor of Poetry from 2013 to 2016.

Samuel Menashe (1925–2011) was born in New York City, the son of Russian-Jewish immigrant parents. He served in the US infantry during the Second World War, and afterwards studied at the Sorbonne in Paris. He returned to New York in the 1950s where, apart from sojourns in Britain, Ireland and Europe, he eked out a living while devoting himself to writing poetry which received very little recognition until he was in his late 70s. His poems are brief in form but profound in their engagement with ultimate questions, with a mysterious simplicity, a spiritual intensity and a lingering emotional force.

Born in Hamburg, **Lisel Mueller** (1924–2020) was an American poet, translator and critic whose family fled Nazi Germany. She arrived in the US in 1939 when she was 15. Her poetry is warm, introspective and apparently simple, concerned above all with people's lives as well as with nature, family, folklore, language, music, memory and history. In 1997 she became was the first German-born poet to win a Pulitzer Prize for Poetry – for *Alive Together: New and Selected Poems* (1996), praised by the judges as 'a testament to the miraculous power of language to interpret and transform our world […] that invites readers to share her vision of experiences we all have in common: sorrow, tenderness, desire, the revelations of art, and mortality – "the hard, dry smack of death against the glass".'

Taha Muhammad Ali (1931–2011) was a much celebrated Palestinian poet whose work was driven by a storyteller's vivid imagination, disarming humour and unflinching honesty. Born in rural Galilee, Muhammad Ali was left without a home when his village was destroyed during the Arab-Israeli war of 1948. Out of this history of shared loss and survival, he created art of the first order. His poems portray experiences ranging from catastrophe to splendour, all the while preserving an essential human dignity. A year after his family were forced to flee for their lives, they slipped back across the border and settled in Nazareth, where he lived until his death in 2011. An autodidact, he owned a souvenir shop now run by his sons near Nazareth's Church of the Annunciation.

Boris A. Novak (*b*. 1953) is a Slovene poet, playwright, translator and author for children. He teaches Comparative Literature at the University of Ljubljana. From the 1970s onwards Novak was active in the movement for the democratisation of society and the freedom of expression. Working with International PEN he organised humanitarian help for refugees from former Yugoslavia and writers from Sarajevo during the war. He has published 100 books (30 in other languages) as well as translating poetry from ten languages into Slovene.

Naomi Shihab Nye (*b*. 1952) is an Arab American writer, anthologist, educator and 'wandering poet'. Born to a Palestinian father and an American mother, she has published over 20 books. She gives voice to her experience as an Arab-American through poems about heritage and peace that overflow with a humanitarian spirit. Through her empathetic use of poetic language, she reveals the shining nature of our daily lives, whether writing about everyday life in her inner-city Texan neighbourhood or the daily rituals of Jews and Palestinians in the war-torn Middle East.

Mary O'Donnell (*b*. 1954) is a Monaghan-born Irish poet and fiction-writer who has published eight poetry collections, most recently *Massacre of the Birds* (2021). Her poetry and prose have shown a continuing focus on themes marginalised in previously male-dominated Irish literature: the female body, sexuality, desire, the family and the institutionalisation of motherhood, as well as the dominant role of religious and nationalist iconography in the construction of Irishness.

John O'Donohue (1956–2008) was an Irish poet, priest, philosopher and environmental activist best known for popularising Celtic spirituality in several bestselling books. The primary influences on his work were the German philosophers Hegel and Meister Eckhart. In *Divine Beauty: The Invisible Embrace* (2003) he wrote: 'The poet wants to drink from the well of origin; to write the poem that has not yet been written. In order to enter this level of originality, the poet must reach beyond the chorus of chattering voices that people the surface of a culture.'

Dennis O'Driscoll (1954-2012) was an Irish poet, critic and anthologist who worked as a civil servant from the age of 16. A poet of true humanity, his wittily observant poetry was attuned to the tragedies and comedies of contemporary life. His books include *Troubled Thoughts, Majestic Dreams: Selected Prose Writings* (2001), *Stepping Stones: Interviews with Seamus Heaney* (2008), and his posthumously published *Collected Poems* (2017).

Gregory Orr (*b.* 1947) grew up in the rural Hudson Valley north of New York. At the age of 12, he shot and killed his brother in a hunting accident, an event that powerfully influenced his ideas about trauma, silence and poetry. After his mother's sudden death in Haiti, he worked as a civil rights volunteer, and was kidnapped at gunpoint in rural Alabama and held for a week in solitary confinement. These events of his youth form the basis of his memoir, *The Blessing* (2002), which tells the story of his childhood and how he came to poetry.

Kathleen Ossip is an American poet and writer who has published four collections, most recently *July* (2021), which includes 'The Believer'. She has described in a short essay how the poem came to her on election night in 2016: 'A woman fervently attempts to find some way to hope. In the process she (of course) apotheosises into a fragile and fallible goddess. She sees much, wonders more. She wonders about paradise and reads Dante's *Paradiso*. Goddess-hood doesn't last forever, but it does create change, a fraction of faith, a sliver of hope. I was brought up with religion but had to battle my way to faith and hope (and love, for that matter). That's probably a battle most of us have to undergo in some form or other, and of course it seems hardest when it's most necessary. 'The Believer' records, as close as I could come at the time, my vision of what an imaginative space based on faith, hope, and love – a God, in short – might be like.'

Alicia Ostriker (*b.* 1937) is a poet, feminist critic and activist, the author of 16 poetry collections, and was one of the first poets in America to write and publish poems about motherhood. Other themes explored in her work include time, history, war and politics as well as the healing power of inner spirituality and how traditional religions exclude female spirituality. Joyce Carol Oates called her 'one of those brilliantly provocative and imaginatively gifted contemporaries whose iconoclastic expression, whether in prose or poetry, is essential to our understanding of our American selves'.

Leanne O'Sullivan (*b.* 1983) comes from the Beara peninsula in West Cork, the setting of her poem 'A Healing' from her 2013 collection *The Mining Road*, an elemental landscape both rural and post-industrial. Her poetry celebrates the earth's intoxicating wildness as well as the richness and preciousness of human experience. Her fourth collection, *A Quarter of an Hour* (2018), draws on the experience of helping her husband recover from losing his memory during a coma and not even knowing her when he awoke. It won the inaugural Farmgate Café National Poetry Award 2019.

Linda Pastan (1932–2023) was an American poet of Jewish background who published 15 collections. Her quiet, elegantly simple poems focus on themes such as family, marriage, parenting and grief, finding beauty or sometimes painful reminders in ordinary moments and exploring and anxieties under the surface of everyday life.

Portugal's **Fernando Pessoa** (1888–1935) lived in Lisbon for most of his life, and died in obscurity there, but is now recognised as one of the most innovative and radical literary figures in modern poetry. He wrote under numerous "heteronyms", literary alter egos with their own identities and writing styles, who supported and criticised each other in the literary journals.

Maya C. Popa (*b.* 1989) is a Romanian-American poet, academic and editor, the daughter of refugees, currently based in New York where she teaches at NYU. In 2018 she became the first woman to serve as the poetry editor of *Publishers Weekly*, the largest international literary trade publication. She has published two collections, *American Faith* (2019) and *Wound is the Origin of Wonder* (2022 US/2023 UK). Her Masters and PhD research showed how heightened states of attention, induced by crises of faith and by wonder spurred Romantic and Victorian poets to generate formally innovative works.

Ai Qing (1910–96) was a visionary Chinese poet whose innovatively adapted free verse was influential in the development of modern Chinese poetry. He studied painting in Paris from 1928 to 1932, but was imprisoned on his return to China for his radical activities. Later he became close to Mao Zedong but fell out of favour and was sentenced to hard labour and exiled to a remote part of the country known as 'Little Siberia' along with his family including his son, Ai Weiwei. His sincerely expressed and defiantly optimistic poetry portrays a country convulsed by change, its legacy of feudalism and imperialism giving way to an uncertain future.

Roger Robinson (*b.* 1967) is a poet and musician born in London to Trinidadian parents. His family moved back to Trinidad when he was four, and he grew up there, returning to London when he was 19. His collection *A Portable Paradise* won both the T.S. Eliot Prize and the Ondaatje Prize. His poems express a fierce anger against injustice, but also convey the irrepressible sense that Robinson cannot help but love people for their humour, oddity and generosity of spirit. He is co-founder of both Spoke Lab and the international writing collective Malika's Kitchen, and is the lead vocalist and lyricist for King Midas Sound.

Tuvia Ruebner (1924–2019) was an Israeli poet who wrote in Hebrew and German. Born in Slovakia, he managed to leave for Palestine in 1941, avoiding the fate of his family who were murdered in Auschwitz. He later lost his first wife Ada in a car accident in 1950 which left him severely injured, followed by his son, Moran, who disappeared during a trip to Ecuador in 1983. Much of his poetry relates to that tragic personal history of family loss and genocidal trauma. His translator Rachel Tzvia Back has written that Ruebner's poetry of 'textual rupture and fragmentation' reflects the extreme rupture and fragmentation of his life, and that his 'insistence on indeterminacy' in his writing 'reflects the indeterminacy of a new life built in the shadows of the old'.

Muriel Rukeyser (1913–80) was one of the most significant and influential American poets of the 20th century. As a young journalist she witnessed events which were to make a serious impact on her life and poetry, including the Scottsboro trial in Alabama, the Gauley Bridge tragedy in West Virginia, and the civil war in Spain. Her poetry confronts the turbulent currents of modern history as it explores with depth and honesty the realms of politics, sexuality, mythic imagination, technological change and family life. She held a visionary belief in the human capacity to create social change through language, and earned an international reputation as a powerful voice against enforced silences of all kind, against the violence of war, poverty and racism.

Elena Shvarts (1948–2010) stood outside all schools and movements in contemporary Russian poetry. She once famously described poetry as a 'dance without legs'. Her own poetry fits this description perfectly, a combination of deeply rhythmic and lyrical dance with the eccentric, perpetual movement of flight. The world of her poems is strange and grotesque; often the setting is urban, but unrecognisable – towns emptied of the everyday and peopled only by animals, spirits and strange elemental forces. A peculiar religious fervour illuminates these scenes, but her religion was unorthodox and highly individual.

Peter Sirr (*b*. 1960) is a leading Irish poet and translator who has published ten poetry collections, a *Selected Poems*, and *Intimate City* (2021), a book of essays on Dublin past and present reflecting his obsessive attachment to the city he has explored repeatedly in many of his poems, including his sequence 'Carmina' which has the scurrilous Latin poet walking the streets of Dublin. In 2016 he published *Sway*, versions of poems by the medieval troubadour poets with whom he clearly shows an affinity in his own poetry, which is both lyrical and adventurous in the tradition of European poetry. He is married to the poet Enda Wyley with whom he presents the highly engaging podcast *Books for Breakfast*.

Edith Södergran (1892-1923) is now regarded as Finland's greatest modern poet, a mystic modernist whose startlingly original poetry (written in Swedish) transcends the limits imposed by her lifelong struggle against TB. But when she died in poverty at 31, Södergran had been dismissed as a mad, megalomaniac aristocrat by most of her Finnish contemporaries.

The driving force of her poetry was her struggle against TB, which she contracted in 1908. For much of her short life she was a semi-invalid in sanatoria in Finland and Switzerland. She saw herself as an inspired free spirit of a new order, a disciple on her own terms of Nietzsche, then of the nature mystic Rudolf Steiner, and finally of Christ. But her voice is subtle and wholly original. It transcends the limits imposed by her illness to make lyrical statements about the violence and darkness of the modern world.

We included her poem 'Hope' [115] in *Soul Food* but wanted to reprint it in *Soul Feast* in a series of poems about hope.

Marin Sorescu (1936–96) was a cheerfully melancholic comic genius, and one of the most original voices in Romanian literature. His mischievous poetry and satirical plays earned him great popularity during the Communist era. While his witty, ironic parables were not overtly critical of the régime, Romanians used to a culture of double-speak could read other meanings in his playful mockery of the human condition. Like Miroslav Holub in Czechoslovakia, Sorescu used plain, deceptively straightforward language, believing that poetry should be 'concise, almost algebraic'. Seamus Heaney wrote that behind Sorescu's 'throwaway charm and poker-faced subversiveness…there is a persistent solidarity with the unregarded life of the ordinary citizen, a willingness to remain at eye-level and on a speaking terms with common experience'.

William Stafford (1914–93) was a much loved American poet. His contemplative poetry celebrates human virtues and universal mysteries, with nature, war, technology and Native American people as his abiding themes. In a typical Stafford poem he seeks an almost sacred place in the wilderness untouched by man, finding meaning in the quest itself and its implications.

Ruth Stone (1915–2011) lived in rural Vermont for much of her life. After her husband's suicide in 1959, she had to raise three daughters alone, all the time writing what she called her 'love poems, all written to a dead man' who forced her to 'reside in limbo' with her daughters. She only won wide recognition for her work in her late 80s, and was still writing poetry of extraordinary variety and radiance well into her 90s – fierce feminist and political poems and hilarious send-ups, meditations on ageing, love and loss.

Interviewed about how she wrote, she responded: 'I wrote my first poem without knowing I'd done it – and found that poems came with this mysterious feeling, a kind of peculiar ecstasy. I'd feel and hear a poem coming from a long way off, like a thunderous train of air.

I'd feel it physically. I'd run like hell to the house, blindly groping for pencil and paper. And then the poem would write itself. I'd write it down from the inside out. The thing knew itself already. There were other times when I'd almost miss it, feeling it pass through me just as I was grabbing the pencil, but then I'd catch it by its tail and pull it backwards into my body. Then the poem came out backwards and I'd have to turn it round.'

Arundhathi Subramaniam (*b.* 1967) is an Indian writer whose poems explore various ambivalences – around human intimacy with its bottlenecks and surprises, life in a Third World megalopolis, myth, the politics of culture and gender, and the persistent trope of the existential journey. As well as four collections of poetry, her books include *The Book of Buddha* (2005) and *Sadhguru: More Than a Life* (2010), *Pilgrim's India: An Anthology* (2011) and *Eating God: A Book of Bhakti Poetry* (2014).

May Swenson (1913–89) was born in Utah to Swedish immigrant parents, growing up with English as her second language, her family speaking mostly Swedish at home. She moved to New York City in 1935, working at a variety of jobs, and not publishing her first collection until 1954. Her highly individual poetry is notable for its adventurous word play, precise and beguiling imagery, eccentric typography and erotic exuberance. The poet Grace Schulman said of her work: 'Questions are the wellspring of May Swenson's art… In her speculations and her close observations, she fulfils Marianne Moore's formula for the working artist: "Curiosity, observation, and a great deal of joy in the thing".' – nowhere more so than in the poem 'Question' which we have selected.

Toon Tellegen (*b.* 1941) is a leading Dutch poet as well as a novelist and children's author. He worked as a GP until his retirement. His tragicomic poems convey human predicaments with great economy and vitality, often rendering them in the form of dramatic stories or dreamlike events, as in 'I drew a line…'

Rosemary Tonks (1928–2014) was a colourful figure in the London literary scene during the 1960s. Her later "disappearance" was one of the literary world's most tantalising mysteries. After publishing two extraordinary poetry collections – and six satirical novels – she turned her back on the literary world. A series of personal tragedies and medical crises made her question the value of literature and embark on a restless, self-torturing spiritual quest. This involved totally renouncing poetry, and suppressing her own books.

Interviewed earlier in 1967, she spoke of her direct literary forebears as Baudelaire and Rimbaud: 'They were both poets of the modern metropolis as we know it and no one has bothered to learn what there is to be learned from them… The main duty of the poet is to excite – to send the senses reeling.' Her poetry is exuberantly sensuous, a hymn to 1960s hedonism set amid the bohemian nighttime world of a London reinvented through French poetic influences and sultry Oriental imagery.

The winner of the Nobel Prize in Literature in 2011, Sweden's **Tomas Tranströmer** (1931–2015) was Scandinavia's best-known and most influential contemporary poet, and worked as a psychologist for 30 years. His poems are often explorations of the borderland between sleep and waking, between the conscious and unconscious states. Many use compressed description and concentrate on a single distinct image as a catalyst for psychological insight and metaphysical interpretation. This acts as a meeting-point or threshold between conflicting elements or forces: sea and land, man and nature, freedom and control, as in the poem 'Alone' [78].

The poet and mystic **Tukaram** (1608–49) is widely regarded as the greatest writer in the Marathi language. In *Eating God: A Book of Bhakti Poetry* (2014), Arundhathi Subramaniam describes how he disappeared at the age of 41, leaving behind nearly 5000 poems or *abhangas*: 'Tukaram wrote a colloquial Marathi verse in praise of Lord Vitthal (Vishnu) – his choice of language and his low caste constituting "a double encroachment on brahmin monopoly", as his translator Dilip Chitre points out. The manuscript of his poems on display in the Vithoba temple in his native village, Dehu, is the same one that is believed to have miraculously surfaced, absolutely intact, thirteen days after orthodox Brahmins forced him to sink it in the local river Indrayani.' Mahatma Gandhi read and translated Tukaram's poetry in jail (along with *Upanishads, Bhagavad Gita* and poems by other Bhakti movement poet-saints) when imprisoned by the British colonial government for his non-violent protests.

Chase Twichell (*b*. 1950) is an American poet and was founder-editor of Ausable Press. She was a Zen Buddhist student of John Daido Loori at Zen Mountain Monastery in the Catskills and has said of her two disciplines: 'Zazen and poetry are both studies of the mind. I find the internal pressure exerted by emotion and by a koan to be similar in surprising and unpredictable ways. Zen is a wonderful sieve through which to pour a poem. It strains out whatever's inessential.'

Lynne Wycherley was born in 1962 by the Fens, a haunting landscape that influenced her poems. She describes her poetry as 'a kind of love poetry, whether for people or places, wild creatures, or stars… It is also a rebellion against reductionism: light, both metaphysical and physical, permeates my imagination and my words.' For some years, she worked in Merton College, Oxford. Later, based in Devon, she helped to raise awareness of the suppressed risks associated with the modern digital world – to children, ecology, and ourselves. Today, she continues to live between the lanterns of sun, fox, owl and moon.

Lee Young-ju is a contemporary South Korean poet. In her prose poems she sketches elemental, deeply surreal scenes with creative energy and a goth-like sensibility. Ryo Yamaguchi has commented: 'These poems call to mind the plays of Samuel Beckett, paintings by Francis Bacon, and films such as Nobuhiko *Obayashi's House*, but in the end they realise a highly original horror, one that allows the reader to observe their own anxiety as separate, an entity apart, like the various elements in Young-ju's elaborate scenes. What these poems offer, among other things, is a chance to grapple with our estrangement from the dead.'

Adam Zagajewski (1945–2021) was born in Lwów (or Lvov, later Lviv), a largely Polish city that became part of the Ukraine shortly after his birth. His ethnic Polish family, who had lived for centuries in Lwów, were then forcibly repatriated to Poland. He came to prominence as a leading figure in Poland's Generation of '68 or *Nowa Fala* (New Wave), and was later active in the Solidarity movement. His luminous, searching poems are imbued by a deep engagement with history, art, music and life.

ACKNOWLEDGEMENTS

The poems in this anthology are reprinted from the following books, all by permission of the publishers listed unless stated otherwise. Thanks are due to all the copyright holders cited below for their kind permission:

Doug Anderson: 'Homage to Li Po' from *Undress, She Said* (Four Way Books, 2022), by permission of The Permissions Company, LLC on behalf of Four Way Books. **Mona Arshi**: 'Little Prayer' from *Dear Big Gods* (Pavilion/Liverpool University Press, 2019). **Stanisław Baranczak**: 'If china', tr. Magnus J. Krynski, from *Selected Poems: The Weight of the Body* (Northwestern University Press, 1989), originally published in *Triquarterly*, an imprint of Northwestern University Press, by permission of the author's estate. **Ellen Bass**: 'Any Common Desolation', from *Indigo* (Copper Canyon Press, 2020), originally published in *Poem-a-Day*, by permission of The Permissions Company, LLC on behalf of Copper Canyon Press; 'The Thing Is' from *The Mules of Love* (BOA Editions, 2002), by permission of The Permissions Company, LLC on behalf of BOA Editions. **Jorge Luis Borges**: 'Poem Written in a Copy of *Beowulf*', tr. Alastair Reid, from *Jorge Luis Borges: Selected Poems,* ed. Alexander Coleman (Penguin Books, 1999). **Lucie Brock-Boido**: 'Soul Keeping Company' from *Soul Keeping Company* (Carcanet Press, 2010). **Jericho Brown**: 'Crossing' from *The Tradition* (Copper Canyon Press, USA, 2019; Picador, UK, 2019), by permission of The Permissions Company, LLC on behalf of Copper Canyon Press.

Edip Cansever: 'Table' from *Edip Cansever: Dirty August*, tr. Julia Clare Tillinghast & Richard Tillinghast (Talisman House, USA, 2009), by permission of the translators. **Giorgio Caproni**: 'Prayer', tr. Peter Sirr, from Giorgio Caproni: *Tutte le poesie* (Garzanti, 2016), by permission of the translator. **Mary Jean Chan**: 'Conversation with a Fantasy Mother', from *Flèche* (Faber & Faber, 2019). **Chen Chen**: 'small book of questions chapter vii' from *Your Emergency Contact Has Experienced an Emergency* (Bloodaxe Books, 2022). **Julius Chingono**: 'As I Go' © 1994, Julius Chingono, first published by *Poetry International* in a special Zimbabwean edition, 10 June 2011, https://www.poetryinternational.com/en/poets-poems/poems/poem/103-11916_AS-I-GO, reprinted here by kind permission of Mrs Juliet Mbofana Chingono and Leonard Dirau (2023). **Sandra**

permission of The Gallery Press, Loughcrew, Oldcastle, Co. Meath, Ireland; 'We Go On' from *We Go On* (Bloodaxe Books, 2024). **Joy Harjo:** 'I Am a Prayer' from *The New Yorker*, 27 November 2023, copyright © 2023, by permission of The Wylie Agency (UK) Limited. **Michael D. Higgins:** 'The Well 2' from *An Arid Season: New Poems* (New Island Books, 2014), by kind permission of the author through the Jonathan Williams Literary Agency. **Edward Hirsch:** 'I Was Never Able to Pray' from the *Northwest Review*, Vol. 48, No. 2, 2010, by permission of Edward Hirsch and the publisher. **Jack Hirschman:** 'Path' by kind permission of the author's estate. **Jane Hirshfield:** 'A Cedary Fragrance', 'The Envoy', 'The Supple Deer' and 'Counting, New Year's Morning, What Powers Yet Remain to Me' from *The Asking: New & Selected Poems* (Bloodaxe Books, 2024). **Miroslav Holub:** The door, tr. Ian Milner, from *Poems Before & After: Collected English Translations*, second edition (Bloodaxe Books, 2006). **A.E. Housman:** 'Good creatures…' from *The Collected Poems* (Jonathan Cape, 1939), out of copyright. **Marie Howe:** 'Postscript' from *What the Earth Seemed to Say: New & Selected Poems* (Bloodaxe Books, 2024). **Langston Hughes:** 'Dreams' and 'Harlem [2]' from *The Collected Poems of Langston Hughes* (Alfred A. Knopf, Inc, 1994), by permission of David Higham Associates.

Noriko Ibaragi: 'When I Was at My Most Beautiful' and 'Your Own Sensitivity at Least' from Y*our Own Sensitivity at Least: Selected Poems of Noriko Ibaragi*, tr. Andrew Houwen & Peter Robinson, unpublished MS, originals © Estate of Noriko Ibaragi, by permission of the translators. **Jeong Ho-seung:** 'A Spider' and 'To Daffodils' from *Though flowers fall I have never forgotten you*, tr. Brother Anthony of Taizé and Susan Hwang (Seoul Selection USA Inc., 2016), by permission of the translators.

Vincent Katz: 'This Beautiful Bubble' from *Resist Much/Obey Little* (Spuyten Duyvil, 2017). **Brendan Kennelly:** 'Permission' and 'Good Souls, to Survive' from *Familiar Strangers: New & Selected Poems 1960-2004* (Bloodaxe Books, 2004). **John Koethe:** 'Lives' from *Beyond Belief* (Farrar, Straus and Giroux, 2022). **Arun Kolatkar:** 'Yeshwant Rao' from *Collected Poems in English*, ed. Arvind Krishna Mehotra (Bloodaxe Books, 2010). **Ted Kooser:** 'November 12, 4:30 a.m.' from *Winter Morning Walks: One Hundred Postcards to Jim Harrison* (Carnegie Mellon University Press, 2000).

Ivan V. Lalic: 'The Spaces of Hope', tr. Francis R. Jones, from *The Passionate Measure*,

of a Relationship' from *Benedictus: A Book of Blessings* (Bantam Books, 2007), by kind permission of Penguin Random House UK. **Dennis O'Driscoll**: 'Fabrications' from *Collected Poems* (Carcanet Press, 2017). **Gregory Orr**: 'To be alive: not just the carcass' from *Concerning the Book That Is the Body of the Beloved* (Copper Canyon Press, 2005), copyright © 2005 by Gregory Orr, by permission of The Permissions Company, LLC on behalf of Copper Canyon Press, www. coppercanyonpress.org. **Kathleen Ossip**: 'The Believer' from *July* (Sarabande Books, 2021), reprinted with the permission of the author. **Alice Ostriker**: 'Wrinkly Lady Dancer' from *The Little Space: Poems Selected and New, 1968–1998* (University of Pittsburgh Press, 1998). **Leanne O'Sullivan**: 'A Healing' from *The Mining Road* (Bloodaxe Books, 2013).

Linda Pastan: 'Imaginary Conversation' and 'I Am Learning How to Abandon the World' from *PM/AM: New and Selected Poems* (New York: W.W. Norton & Company, 1982, copyright © 1982 by Linda Pastan, reprinted with the permission of the Jean V. Naggar Agency, Inc. on behalf of the author's estate. **Fernando Pessoa**: 'They Spoke to Me of People, and of Humanity' from *Fernando Pessoa & Co.: Selected Poems*, tr. Richard Zenith (New York: Grove Press, 1998), by permission of the translator. **Maya C. Popa**: 'Dear Life' from *Wound is the Origin of Wonder* (Picador, 2023) by permission of the author.

Ai Qing: 'The Lamp', tr. Robert Dorsett, from *Ai Qing: Selected Poems*, tr. Robert Dorsett (Crown, an imprint of Random House, 2021), by permission of Penguin Random House.

Roger Robinson: 'A Portable Paradise' from *A Portable Paradise* (Peepal Tree Press, 2019). **Tuvia Ruebner**: 'Wonder' from *In the Illuminated Dark: Selected Poems of Tuvia Ruebner*, tr. Rachel Tzvia Back. (Hebrew Union College Press and the University of Pittsburgh Press, 2015), by permission of the translator. **Muriel Rukeyser**: 'Yes' from *Selected Poems*, ed. Adrienne Rich (Bloodaxe Books, 2013).

Elena Shvarts: 'Set your course by the Sun…', tr. Sasha Dugdale, from *Birdsong on the Seabed*, tr. Sasha Dugdale (Bloodaxe Books, 2008). Peter Sirr: 'A Saxon Primer' from *The Swerve* (The Gallery Press, 2023), by permission of The Gallery Press, Loughcrew, Oldcastle, Co. Meath, Ireland. Edith Södergran: 'Hope', tr. David McDuff, from *Complete Poems*, tr. David McDuff (Bloodaxe Books, 1984). **Marin**

Sorescu: 'With Only One Life', tr. D.J. Enright & Ioana Russell-Gebbett from *The Biggest Egg in the World*, tr. Ioana Russell-Gebbett with various translators (Bloodaxe Books, 1987). **William Stafford:** 'The Way It Is' and 'Listening' from *Ask Me: 100 Essential Poems*, copyright 1954, © 1991, 1998 by William Stafford and the Estate of William Stafford, by permission of The Permissions Company, LLC on behalf of Graywolf Press, Minneapolis, Minnesota, graywolfpress.org. **Ruth Stone:** 'Train Ride' from *What Love Comes To: New & Selected Poems* (Bloodaxe Books, 2009). **Arundhathi Subramaniam:** 'Prayer' from *Where I Live: New & Selected Poems* (Bloodaxe Books, 2009). **May Swenson:** 'Question' from *Nature: Poems Old and New*, copyright © 1994 by May Swenson, reprinted with the permission of Houghton Mifflin Company.

Toon Tellegen: 'I drew a line…' tr. Judith Wilkinson, from *About Love and About Nothing Else*, tr. Judith Wilkinson (Shoestring Press, 2008). **Rosemary Tonks:** 'Addiction to an Old Mattress' from *Bedouin of the London Evening: Collected Poems & Selected Prose*, second edition (Bloodaxe Books, 2014). **Tomas Tranströmer:** 'After Someone's Death', 'Tracks' and 'Alone' from *New Collected Poems*, tr. Robin Fulton (Bloodaxe Books, 2011). **Tukaram:** 'When He comes…', tr. Dilip Chitre, from *Says Tuka: Selected Poetry of Tukaram* (Penguin Books India, 1991), by permission of the estate of Dilip Chitre and Poetrywala, India. **Chase Twichell:** 'Saint Animal' from *Horses Where the Answers Should Have Been: New & Selected Poems* (Bloodaxe Books, 2010).

Lynne Wycherley: 'The Substitute Sky' from *Soul of the Earth: The Awen Anthology of Eco-spiritual Poetry* (Awen Publications, 2011), by permission of the author Lynne Wycherley.

Lee Young-ju: 'Lumberjack Diary', tr. Jae Kim, from *Poetry* (April 2021), by permission of the translator.

Adam Zagajewski: 'Wake Up', tr. Clare Cavanagh, from *Asymmetry*, tr. Clare Cavanagh (Farrar, Straus and Giroux, 2014).

Every effort has been made to trace copyright holders of the poems published in this book. The editors and publisher apologise if any material has been included without permission or without the appropriate acknowledgement, and would be glad to be told of anyone who has not been consulted.

INDEX OF WRITERS

[translations and notes in italics]